THE
PRINCE

Niccolò Machiavelli

Translated and
with an Introduction by

Harvey C. Mansfield

Second Edition

THE UNIVERSITY OF CHICAGO PRESS
Chicago and London

The University of Chicago Press, Chicago 60637
The University of Chicago Press, Ltd., London

©1985, 1998 by The University of Chicago
All rights reserved. Second edition 1998.
Printed in the United States of America

20 19 18 17 16   14

ISBN-13: 978-0-226-50044-7 (paper)
ISBN-10: 0-226-50044-6 (paper)

LIBRARY OF CONGRESS CATALOGING-IN-PUBLICATION DATA

Machiavelli, Niccolò, 1469–1527.
    [Principe. English]
    The prince / Niccolò Machiavelli : translated with an
introduction by Harvey C. Mansfield. — 2nd ed.
        p.   cm.
    Includes bibliographical references and index.
    ISBN 0-226-50043-8 (alk. paper).—ISBN 0-226-
50044-6 (pbk. : alk. paper)
    1. Political science—Early works to 1800.
2. Political ethics—Early works to 1800.   I. Title.
JC143.M38   1998
320.1—dc21   98-5772
                                          CIP

THE
PRINCE

11/28/23 Notes

Fortune

Virtú

★ This book contrary to his advice

Power

Glory

Freedom

Principality
Unfree/
Not used to
Freedom

Republic (i.e. Florence)
Free/Used to Freedom

(20, 21)

Agenda

- Appearances vs. Reality
- Law & Force

Exhortation of Italy

Disarming the People?

Is this satire?

Feared vs. Loved?

Some of Machiavelli's trade-offs & Balances

Being easier to win over enemies than friends

Fotresses: Foreigners vs the people

Prince
More money
more power
hopefully loyalty by
People

Our army
Mercenaries

Family

Grandi
Money &
Power

[Numbers (population)]

Contents

Introduction

Anyone who picks up Machiavelli's *The Prince* holds in his hands the most famous book on politics ever written. Its closest rival might be Plato's *Republic,* but that book discusses politics in the context of things above politics, and politics turns out to have a limited and subordinate place. In *The Prince* Machiavelli also discusses politics in relation to things outside politics, as we shall see, but his conclusion is very different. Politics according to him is not limited by things above it, and things normally taken to be outside politics—the "givens" in any political situation—turn out to be much more under the control of politics than politicians, peoples, and philosophers have hitherto assumed. Machiavelli's *The Prince,* then, is the most famous book on politics when politics is thought to be carried on for its own sake, unlimited by anything above it. The renown of *The Prince* is precisely to have been the first and the best book to argue that politics has and should have its own rules and should not accept rules of any kind or from any source where the object is not to win or prevail over others. *The Prince* is briefer and pithier than Machiavelli's other major work, *Discourses on Livy,* for *The Prince* is addressed to Lorenzo de' Medici, a prince like the busy executive of our day who has little time for reading. So *The Prince* with its political advice to an active politician that politics should not be limited by anything not political, is by far more famous than the *Discourses on Livy.*

We cannot, however, agree that *The Prince* is the most famous book on politics without immediately correcting this to say that it is the most infamous. It is famous for its infamy, for recommending the kind of politics that ever since has been called Machiavellian. The essence of this politics is that "you can get away with murder": that no divine sanction, or degradation of soul, or twinge of conscience will come to punish you. If you succeed, you will not even have to face the infamy of murder, because when "men acquire who can acquire, they will be praised or not blamed" (Chapter 3). Those criminals who are infamous have merely been on the losing side. Machiavelli and Machiavellian politics are famous or infamous for their willingness to brave infamy.

Yet it must be reported that the prevailing view among scholars of Machiavelli is that he was not an evil man who taught evil doctrines, and that he does not deserve his infamy. With a view to his preference for republics over principalities (more evident in *Discourses on Livy* than in *The Prince*, but not absent in the latter), they cannot believe he was an apologist for tyranny; or, impressed by the sudden burst of Italian patriotism in the last chapter of *The Prince*, they forgive him for the sardonic observations which are not fully consistent with this generous feeling but are thought to give it a certain piquancy (this is the opinion of an earlier generation of scholars); or, on the basis of Machiavelli's saying in Chapter 15 that we should take our bearings from "what is done" rather than from "what should be done," they conclude that he was a forerunner of modern political science, which is not an evil thing because it merely tells us what happens without passing judgment. In sum, the prevailing view of the scholars offers excuses for Machiavelli: he was a republican, a patriot, or a scientist, and therefore, in explicit contradiction to the reaction of most people to Machiavelli as soon as they hear of his doctrines, Machiavelli was not "Machiavellian."

The reader can form his own judgment of these excuses for Machiavelli. I do not recommend them, chiefly because they make Machiavelli less interesting. They transform him into a herald of the future who had the luck to sound the tunes we hear so often today—democracy, nationalism or self-determination, and science. Instead of challenging our favorite beliefs and forcing us to think, Machiavelli is enlisted into a chorus of self-congratulation.

There is, of course, evidence for the excuses supplied on behalf of Machiavelli, and that evidence consists of the excuses offered by Machiavelli himself. If someone were to accuse him of being an apologist for tyranny, he can indeed point to a passage in the *Discourses on Livy* (II 2) where he says (rather carefully) that the common good is not observed unless in republics; but if someone else were to accuse him of supporting republicanism, he could point to the same chapter, where he says that the hardest slavery of all is to be conquered by a republic. And, while he shows his Italian patriotism in Chapter 26 of *The Prince* by exhorting someone to seize Italy in order to free it from the barbarians, he also shows his fairmindedness by advising a French king in Chapter 3 how he might better invade Italy the next time. Lastly, it is true that he sometimes merely reports the evil that he sees, while (unnecessarily) deploring it; but at other times he urges us to share in that evil and he virtuously condemns half-hearted immoralists. Although he was an exceedingly bold writer who seems to have deliberately courted an evil reputation, he was nonetheless not so bold as to fail to provide excuses, or prudent reservations, for his boldest statements. Since I have spoken at length on this point in another place, and will not hesitate to mention the work of Leo Strauss, it is not necessary to explain it further here.

What is at issue in the question of whether Machiavelli was "Machiavellian"? To see that a matter of the highest importance is involved we must not rest satisfied with either scholarly excuses or moral frowns. For the matter at issue is the character of the rules by which we reward human beings with fame or condemn them with infamy, the very status of morality. Machiavelli does not make it clear at first that this grave question is his subject. In the Dedicatory Letter he approaches Lorenzo de' Medici with hat in one hand and *The Prince* in the other. Since, he says, one must be a prince to know the nature of peoples and a man of the people to know the nature of princes, he seems to offer Lorenzo the knowledge of princes he does not have but needs. In accordance with this half-serious promise, Machiavelli speaks about the kinds of principalities in the first part of *The Prince* (Chapters 1–11) and, as we learn of the necessity of conquest, about the kinds of armies in the second part (Chapters 12–14). But at the same time (to make a long story short), we learn that the prince must or may lay his foundations on the people (Chapter 9) and that while his only object should be the art of war, he must in time of peace pay attention to moral qualities in such manner as to be able to use them in time of war (Chapter 14, end).

Thus are we prepared for Machiavelli's clarion call in Chapter 15, where he proclaims that he "departs from the orders of others" and says why. For moral qualities are qualities "held good" by the people; so, if the prince must conquer, and wants, like the Medici, to lay his foundation on the people, who are the keepers of morality, then a new morality consistent with the necessity of conquest must be found, and the prince has to be taught anew about the nature of peoples by Machiavelli. In departing from the orders of others, it appears more fitting to Machiavelli "to go directly to the effectual truth of the thing than to the imagination of it." Many have imagined republics and principalities, but one cannot "let go of what is done for what should be done," because a man who "makes a profession of good in all regards" comes to ruin among so many who are not good. The prince must learn to be able not to be good, and use this ability or not according to necessity.

This concise statement is most efficacious. It contains a fundamental assault on all morality and political science, both Christian and classical, as understood in Machiavelli's time. Morality had meant not only doing the right action, but also doing it for the right reason or for the love of God. Thus, to be good was thought to require "a profession of good" in which the motive for doing good was explained; otherwise, morality would go no deeper than outward conformity to law, or even to superior force, and could not be distinguished from it. But professions of good could not accompany moral actions in isolation from each other; they would have to be elaborated so that moral actions would be consistent with each other and the life of a moral person would form a whole. Such elaboration requires an effort of imagination, since the consistency we see tells us only of the presence of outward conformity, and the elaboration extends over a society, because it is difficult to live a moral life by oneself; hence morality requires the construction of an imagined republic or principality, such as Plato's *Republic* or St. Augustine's *City of God*.

When Machiavelli denies that imagined republics and principalities "exist in truth," and declares that the truth in these or all matters is the effectual truth, he says that no moral rules exist, not made by men, which men must abide by. The rules or laws that exist are those made by governments or other powers acting under necessity, and they must be obeyed out of the same necessity. Whatever is necessary may be called just and reasonable, but justice is no more reasonable than what a person's prudence tells him he must acquire for himself, or must submit to, because men cannot afford justice in any sense that transcends their own preservation. Machiavelli did not attempt (as did Hobbes) to formulate a new definition of justice based on self-preservation. Instead, he showed what he meant by not including justice among the eleven pairs of moral qualities that he lists in Chapter 15. He does mention justice in Chapter 21 as a calculation of what a weaker party might expect from a prince whom it has supported in war, but even this little is contradicted by what Machiavelli says about keeping faith in Chapter 18 and about betraying one's old supporters in Chapter 20. He also brings up justice as something identical with necessity in Chapter 26. But, what is most striking, he never mentions—not in *The Prince*, or in any of his works—natural justice or natural law, the two conceptions of justice in the classical and medieval tradition that had been handed down to his time and that could be found in the writings on this subject of all his contemporaries. The grave issue raised by the dispute whether Machiavelli was truly "Machiavellian" is this: does justice exist by nature or by God, or is it the convenience of the prince (government)? "So let a prince win and maintain a state: the means will always be judged honorable, and will be praised by everyone" (Chapter 18). Reputation, then, is outward conformity to successful human force and has no reference to moral rules that the government might find inconvenient.

If there is no natural justice, perhaps Machiavelli can teach the prince how to rule in its absence—but with a view to the fact that men "profess" it. It does not follow of necessity that because no natural justice exists, princes can rule successfully without it. Governments might be as unsuccessful in making and keeping conquests as in living up to natural justice; indeed, the traditional proponents of natural justice, when less confident of their own cause, had pointed to the uncertainty of gain, to the happy inconstancy of fortune, as an argument against determined wickedness. But Machiavelli thinks it possible to "learn" to be able not to be good. For each of the difficulties of gaining and keeping, even and especially for the fickleness of fortune, he has a "remedy," to use his frequent expression. Since nature or God does not support human justice, men are in need of a remedy; and the remedy is the prince, especially the new prince. Why must the new prince be preferred?

In the heading to the first chapter of *The Prince* we see that the kinds of principalities are to be discussed together with the ways in which they are acquired, and then in the chapter itself we find more than this, that principalities are classified into kinds by the ways in which they are acquired.

"Acquisition," an economic term, is Machiavelli's word for "conquest"; and acquisition determines the classifications of governments, not their ends or structures, as Plato and Aristotle had thought. How is acquisition related to the problem of justice?

Justice requires a modest complement of external goods, the equipment of virtue in Aristotle's phrase, to keep the wolf from the door and to provide for moral persons a certain decent distance from necessities in the face of which morality might falter or even fail. For how can one distribute justly without something to distribute? But, then, where is one to get this modest complement? The easy way is by inheritance. In Chapter 2, Machiavelli considers hereditary principalities, in which a person falls heir to everything he needs, especially the political power to protect what he has. The hereditary prince, the man who has everything, is called the "natural prince," as if to suggest that our grandest and most comprehensive inheritance is what we get from nature. But when the hereditary prince looks upon his inheritance—and when we, generalizing from his case, add up everything we inherit—is it adequate?

The difficulty with hereditary principalities is indicated at the end of Chapter 2, where Machiavelli admits that hereditary princes will have to change but claims that change will not be disruptive because it can be gradual and continuous. He compares each prince's own construction to building a house that is added on to a row of houses: you may not inherit all you need, but you inherit a firm support and an easy start in what you must acquire. But clearly a row of houses so built over generations presupposes that the first house was built without existing support and without an easy start. Inheritance presupposes an original acquisition made without a previous inheritance. And in the original acquisition, full attention to the niceties of justice may unfortunately not be possible. One may congratulate an American citizen for all the advantages to which he is born; but what of the nasty necessities that prepared this inheritance—the British expelled, Indians defrauded, blacks enslaved?

Machiavelli informs us in the third chapter, accordingly, that "truly it is a very natural and ordinary thing to desire to acquire." In the space of a few pages, "natural" has shifted in meaning from hereditary to acquisitive. Or can we be consoled by reference to Machiavelli's republicanism, not so prominent in *The Prince*, with the thought that acquisitiveness may be natural to princes but is not natural to republics? But in Chapter 3 Machiavelli praises the successful acquisitiveness of the "Romans," that is, the Roman republic, by comparison to the imprudence of the king of France. At the time Machiavelli is referring to, the Romans were not weak and vulnerable as they were at their inception; they had grown powerful and were still expanding. Even when they had enough empire to provide an inheritance for their citizens, they went on acquiring. Was this reasonable? It was, because the haves of this world cannot quietly inherit what is coming to them; lest they be treated now as they once treated others, they must keep an eye on the have-nots. To keep a step ahead of the have-nots the haves must think and behave like have-nots. They certainly cannot afford justice to the have-nots, nor can they waste time or money on sympathy.

In the Dedicatory Letter Machiavelli presents himself to Lorenzo as a have-not, "from a low and mean state"; and one thing he lacks besides honorable employment, we learn, is a unified fatherland. Italy is weak and divided. Then should we say that acquisitiveness is justified for Italians of Machiavelli's time, including him? As we have noted, Machiavelli does not seem to accept this justification because, still in Chapter 3, he advises a French king how to correct the errors he had made in his invasion of Italy. Besides, was Machiavelli's fatherland Italy or was it Florence? In Chapter 15 he refers to "our language," meaning

Tuscan, and in Chapter 20 to "our ancients," meaning Florentines. But does it matter whether Machiavelli was essentially an Italian or a Florentine patriot? Anyone's fatherland is defined by an original acquisition, a conquest, and hence is always subject to redefinition of the same kind. To be devoted to one's native country at the expense of foreigners is no more justified than to be devoted to one's city at the expense of fellow countrymen, or to one's family at the expense of fellow city-dwellers, or, to adapt a Machiavellian remark in Chapter 17, to one's patrimony at the expense of one's father. So to "unify" one's fatherland means to treat it as a conquered territory—conquered by a king or republic from within; and Machiavelli's advice to the French king on how to hold his conquests in Italy was also advice to Lorenzo on how to unify Italy. It appears that, in acquiring, the new prince acquires for himself.

What are the qualities of the new prince? What must he do? First, as we have seen, he should rise from private or unprivileged status; he should not have an inheritance, or if he has, he should not rely on it. He should owe nothing to anyone or anything, for having debts of gratitude would make him dependent on others, in the widest sense dependent on fortune. It might seem that the new prince depends at least on the character of the country he conquers, and Machiavelli says at the end of Chapter 4 that Alexander had no trouble in holding Asia because it had been accustomed to the government of one lord. But then in Chapter 5 he shows how this limitation can be overcome. A prince who conquers a city used to living in freedom need not respect its inherited liberties; he can and should destroy such cities or else rule them personally. Fortune supplies the prince with nothing more than opportunity, as when Moses found the people of Israel enslaved by the Egyptians, Romulus found himself exposed at birth, Cyrus found the Persians discontented with the empire of the Medes, and Theseus found the Athenians dispersed (Chapter 6). These famous founders had the virtue to recognize the opportunity that fortune offered to them—opportunity for them, harsh necessity to their peoples. Instead of dispersing the inhabitants of a free city (Chapter 5), the prince is lucky enough to find them dispersed (Chapter 6). This suggests that the prince could go so far as to make his own opportunity by creating a situation of necessity in which no one's inherited goods remain to him and everything is owed to you, the new prince. When a new prince comes to power, should he be grateful to those who helped him get power and rely on them? Indeed not. A new prince has "lukewarm defenders" in his friends and allies, because they expect benefits from him; as we have seen, it is much better to conciliate his former enemies who feared losing everything (compare Chapters 6 and 20).

Thus, the new prince has virtue that enables him to overcome his dependence on inheritance in the widest sense, including custom, nature, and fortune, and that shows him how to arrange it that others depend on him and his virtue (Chapters 9, 24). But if virtue is to do all this, it must have a new meaning. Instead of cooperating with nature or God, as in the various classical and Christian conceptions, virtue must be taught to be acquisitive on its own. Machiavelli teaches the new meaning of virtue by showing us both the new and the old meanings. In a famous passage on the successful criminal Agathocles in Chapter 8, he says "one cannot call it virtue to kill one's citizens, betray one's friends, to be without faith, without mercy, without religion." Yet in the very next sentence Machiavelli proceeds to speak of "the virtue of Agathocles."

The prince, we have seen in Chapter 15, must "learn to be able not to be good, and to use this and not use it according to necessity." Machiavelli supplies this knowledge in Chapters 16 to 18. First, with superb calm, he delivers home-truths concerning the moral virtue of liberality. It is no use being liberal (or generous) unless it is noticed, so that you are "held liberal" or get a name for liberality. But a prince cannot be held liberal by being liberal, because he would have to be liberal to a few by burdening the many with taxes; the many would be offended, the prince would have to retrench, and he would soon get a name for stinginess. The right way to get a reputation for liberality is to begin by not caring about having a reputation for stinginess. When the people see that the prince gets the job done without burdening them, they will in time consider him liberal to them and stingy only to the few to whom he gives nothing. In the event, "liberality" comes to mean taking little rather than giving much.

As regards cruelty and mercy, in Chapter 8 Machiavelli made a distinction between cruelties well used and badly used; well-used cruelties are done once, for self-defense, and not continued but turned to the benefit of one's subjects, and badly used ones continue and increase. In Chapter 17, however, he does not mention this distinction but rather speaks only of using mercy badly. Mercy is badly used when, like the Florentine people in a certain instance, one seeks to avoid a reputation for cruelty and thus allows disorders to continue which might be stopped with a very few examples of cruelty. Disorders harm everybody; executions harm only the few or the one who is executed. As the prince may gain a name for liberality by taking little, so he may be held merciful by not being cruel too often.

Machiavelli's new prince arranges the obligation of his subjects to himself in a manner rather like that of the Christian God, in the eye of whom all are guilty by original sin; hence God's mercy appears less as the granting of benefits than as the remission of punishment. With this thought in mind, the reader will not be surprised that Machiavelli goes on to discuss whether it is better for the prince to be loved or feared. It would be best to be both loved and feared, but, when necessity forces a choice, it is better to be feared, because men love at their convenience but they fear at the convenience of the prince. Friends may fail you, but the dread of punishment will never forsake you. If the prince avoids making himself hated, which he can do by abstaining from the property of others, "because men forget the death of a father more quickly than the loss of a patrimony," he will again have subjects obligated to him for what he does not do to them rather than for benefits he provides.

It is laudable for a prince to keep faith, Machiavelli says in Chapter 18, but princes who have done great things have done them by deceit and betrayal. The prince must learn how to use the beast in man, or rather the beasts; for man is an animal who can be many animals, and he must know how to be a fox as well as a lion. Men will not keep faith with you; how can you keep it with them? Politics, Machiavelli seems to say, as much as consists in breaking promises, for circumstances change and new necessities arise that make it impossible to hold to one's word. The only question is, can one get away with breaking one's promises? Machiavelli's answer is a confident yes. He broadens the discussion, speaking of five moral qualities, especially religion; he says that men judge by appearances and that when one judges by appearances, "one looks to the end." The end is the outcome or the effect, and if a prince wins and maintains a state, the means will always be judged honorable. Since Machiavelli has just emphasized the prince's need to appear religious, we may compare the people's attitude toward a successful prince with their belief in divine providence. As people assume that the outcome of events in the world is determined by God's providence, so they conclude that the means chosen by God cannot have been unworthy. Machiavelli's thought here is both a subtle attack on the notion of divine providence and a subtle appreciation of it, insofar as the prince can appropriate it to his own use.

It is not easy to state exactly what virtue is, according to Machiavelli. Clearly he does not leave virtue as it was in the classical or Christian tradition, nor does he imitate any other writer of his time. Virtue in his new meaning seems to be a prudent or well-taught combination of vice and virtue in the old meaning. Virtue for him is not a mean between two extremes of vice, as is moral virtue for Aristotle. As we have seen, in Chapter 15 eleven virtues (the same number as Aristotle's, though not all of them the same virtues) are paired with eleven vices. From this we might conclude that virtue does not shine of itself, as when it is done for its own sake. Rather, virtue is as it takes effect, its truth is its effectual truth; and it is effectual only when it is seen in contrast to its opposite. Liberality, mercy, and love are impressive only when one expects stinginess (or rapacity), cruelty, and fear. This contrast makes virtue apparent and enables the prince to gain a reputation for virtue. If this is so, then the new meaning Machiavelli gives to virtue, a meaning which makes use of vice, must not entirely replace but somehow continue to coexist with the old meaning, according to which virtue is shocked by vice.

A third quality of the new prince is that he must make his own foundations. Although to be acquisitive means to be acquisitive for oneself, the prince cannot do everything with his own hands: he needs help from others. But in seeking help he must take account of the "two diverse humors" to be found in every city—the people, who desire not to be commanded or oppressed by the great, and the great, who desire to command and oppress the people (Chapter 9). Of these two humors, the prince should choose the people. The people are easier to satisfy, too inert to move against him, and too numerous to kill, whereas the great regard themselves as his equals, are ready and able to conspire against him, and are replaceable.

The prince, then, should ally with the people against the aristocracy; but how should he get their support? Machiavelli gives an example in the conduct of Cesare Borgia, whom he praises for the foundations he laid (Chapter 7).

When Cesare had conquered the province of Romagna, he installed "Remirro de Orco" (actually a Spaniard, Don Remiro de Lorqua) to carry out a purge of the unruly lords there. Then, because Cesare thought Remirro's authority might be excessive, and his exercise of it might become hateful—in short, because Remirro had served his purpose—he purged the purger and one day had Remirro displayed in the piazza at Cesena in two pieces. This spectacle left the people "at once satisfied and stupefied"; and Cesare set up a more constitutional government in Romagna. The lesson: constitutional government is possible but only after an unconstitutional beginning.

In Chapter 9 Machiavelli discusses the "civil principality," which is gained through the favor of the people, and gives as example Nabis, "prince" of the Spartans, whom he calls a tyrant in the *Discourses on Livy* because of the crimes Nabis committed against his rivals. In Chapter 8 Machiavelli considers the principality that is attained through crimes, and cites Agathocles and Oliverotto, both of whom were very popular despite their crimes. As one ponders these two chapters, it becomes more and more difficult to find a difference between gaining a principality through crimes and through the favor of the people. Surely Cesare Borgia, Agathocles, and Nabis seemed to have followed the same policy of pleasing the people by cutting up the great. Finally, in Chapter 19, Machiavelli reveals that the prince need not have the support of the people after all. Even if he is hated by the people (since in fact he cannot fail to be hated by someone), he can, like the Roman emperor Severus, make his foundation with his soldiers (see also Chapter 20). Severus had such virtue, Machiavelli says, with an unobtrusive comparison to Cesare Borgia in Chapter 7, that he "stupefied" the people and "satisfied" the soldiers.

Fourth, the new prince has his own arms, and does not rely on mercenary or auxiliary armies. Machiavelli omits a discussion of the laws a prince should establish, in contrast to the tradition of political science, because, he says, "there cannot be good laws where there are not good arms, and where there are good arms there must be good laws" (Chapter 12). He speaks of the prince's arms in Chapters 12 to 14, and in Chapter 14 he proclaims that the prince should have no other object or thought but the art of war. He must be armed, since it is quite unreasonable for one who is armed to obey one who is unarmed. With this short remark Machiavelli seems to dismiss the fundamental principle of classical political science, the rule of the wise, not to mention the Christian promise that the meek shall inherit the earth.

Machiavelli does not mean that those with the most bodily force always win, for he broadens the art of war to include the acquisition as well as the use of arms. A prince who has no army but has the art of war will prevail over one with an army but without the art. Thus, to be armed means to know the art of war, to exercise it in time of peace, and to have read histories about great captains of the past. In this regard Machiavelli mentions Xenophon's "Life of Cyrus," as he calls it (actually "The Education of Cyrus"), the first and best work in the literature of "mirrors of princes" to which *The Prince* belongs. But he calls it a history, not a mirror of princes, and says that it inspired the Roman general Scipio, whom he criticizes in Chapter 17 for excessive mercy. Not books of imaginary republics and principalities, or treatises on law, but histories of war, are recommended reading for the prince.

Last, the new prince with his own arms is his own master. The deeper meaning of Machiavelli's slogan, "one's own arms," is religious, or rather, antireligious. If man is obligated to God as his creature, then man's own necessities are subordinate or even irrelevant to his most pressing duties. It would not matter if he could not afford justice: God commands it! Thus Machiavelli must look at the new prince who is also a prophet, above all at Moses. Moses was a "mere executor of things that had been ordered for him by God" (Chapter 6); hence he should be admired for the grace that made him worthy of speaking with God. Or should it be said, as Machiavelli says in Chapter 26, that Moses had "virtue," the virtue that makes a prince dependent on no one but himself? In Chapter 13 Machiavelli retells the biblical story of David and Goliath to illustrate the necessity of one's own arms. When Saul offered his arms to David, David refused them, saying, according to Machiavelli, that with them he could not give a good account of himself, and according to the Bible, that the Lord "will deliver me out of the hand of this Philistine." Machiavelli also gives David a knife to go with his sling, the knife which according to the Bible he took from the fallen Goliath and used to cut off his head.

Must the new prince—the truly new prince—then be his own prophet and make a new religion so as to be his own master? The great power of religion can be seen in what Moses and David founded, and in what Savonarola nearly accomplished in Machiavelli's own time and city. The unarmed prince whom he disparages in Chapter 6 actually disposes of formidable weapons necessary to the art of war. The unarmed prophet becomes armed if he uses religion for his own purposes rather than God's; and because the prince cannot acquire glory for himself without bringing order to his principality, using religion for himself is using it to answer human necessities generally.

The last three chapters of *The Prince* take up the question of how far man can make his own world. What are the limits set on Machiavelli's political science (or the "art of war") by fortune? At the end of Chapter 24 he blames "these princes of ours" who accuse fortune for their troubles and not their own indolence. In quiet times they do not take account of the storm to come, but they should—they can. They believe that the people will be disgusted by the arrogance of the foreign conquerors and will call them back. But "one should never fall in the belief you can find someone to pick you up." Whether successful or not, such a defense is base, because it does not depend on you and your virtue.

With this high promise of human capability, Machiavelli introduces his famous Chapter 25 on fortune. He begins it by asking how much of the world is governed by fortune and God, and how much by man. He then supposes that half is governed by fortune (forgetting God) and half by man, and he compares fortune to a violent river that can be contained with dikes and dams. Turning to particular men, he shows that the difficulty in containing fortune lies in the inability of one who is impetuous to succeed in quiet times or of one who is cautious to succeed in stormy times. Men, with their fixed natures and habits, do not vary as the times vary, and so they fall under the control of the times, of fortune. Men's fixed natures are the special problem, Machiavelli indicates; so the problem of overcoming the influence of fortune reduces to the problem of overcoming the fixity of different human natures. Having a fixed nature is what makes one liable to changes of fortune. Pope Julius II succeeded because the times were in accord with his impetuous nature; if he had lived longer, he would have come to grief. Machiavelli blames him for his inflexibility, and so implies that neither he nor the rest of us need respect the natures or natural inclinations we have been given.

What is the new meaning of virtue that Machiavelli has developed but flexibility according to the times or situation? Yet, though one should learn to be both impetuous and cautious (these stand for all the other contrary qualities), on the whole one should be impetuous. Fortune is a woman who "lets herself be won more by the impetuous than by those who proceed coldly"; hence she is a friend of the young. He makes the politics of the new prince appear in the image of rape; impetuous himself, Machiavelli forces us to see the question he has raised about the status of morality. Whether he says what he appears to say about the status of women may be doubted, however. The young men who master Lady Fortune come with audacity and leave exhausted, but she remains ageless, waiting for the next ones. One might go so far as to wonder who is raping whom, cautiously as it were, and whether Machiavelli, who has personified fortune, can impersonate her in the world of modern politics he attempted to create.

HARVEY C. MANSFIELD

A Note on the Translation

In this translation I have sought to be as literal and exact as is consistent with readable English. Since I am convinced that Machiavelli was one of the greatest and subtlest minds to whom we have access, I take very seriously the translator's obligation to present a writer's thought in his own words, insofar as possible. It did not seem to me my duty, therefore, to find a rough equivalent to Machiavelli's words in up-to-date, colloquial prose, and to avoid cognates at all costs. For example, I am not embarrassed to translate *provincia* "province" and *patria* "fatherland" because these English words are perfectly intelligible even though they are not the expressions we would use today. It is worthwhile trying to retain the connotations of those words as Machiavelli used them, as well as trying to avoid the connotations of their modern equivalents, such as "nation." With this intent in translation, I have tried to retain some flavor of Machiavelli's style by preserving his favorite expressions and some of his crowded sentences and difficult grammar. If the result seems a little old-fashioned, so it should. Machiavelli's text will live without our help, and it will die if we suffocate it with the sort of hospitality that allows it to live with us only on our terms.

As to exactness, I would have liked never to vary the translation of such important words as *impresa, modo,* and *respetto,* but I found it impossible to produce a readable version with such a rule. I have kept *virtù* as "virtue," so that readers of this translation can follow and join the dispute over the meaning Machiavelli attaches to the word. If his use of it sounds strange, as it did when he wrote and still does today, then let the reader wonder at finding something strange. It is not the translator's business to make everything familiar.

For some of my departures from consistency, I have noted the literal meaning in the notes. I have surely not varied the translation merely for the sake of elegance. We should not be so certain that we know what Machiavelli's key terms or concepts are. Frequently he will use a word or phrase several times in close proximity, and such density of usage can alert us to the importance of that word in that context. His pronouns are often ambiguous in their reference, and I have sometimes had to make a choice that he leaves open. I have indicated in the notes the occasions on which Machiavelli departs from his usual familiar "you" and addresses a formal or plural "you," a "you" who is asked to see, consider, or think something.

In the spirit of accuracy, I have not provided long historical notes to explain Machiavelli's examples. *The Prince* is not a history book. It was written, we believe, in 1513, and it was dedicated, we know, to Lorenzo de' Medici. But it was written for the future and addressed above all others, including Lorenzo, to "whoever understands it" (Chapter 15). This does not mean that readers who want to understand *The Prince* can ignore Machiavelli's examples and merely make a list of his sensational assertions. On the contrary, those assertions are always modified, sometimes even contradicted, by the examples. But the examples will not serve as examples if the reader does not look carefully at the information Machiavelli gives him. He may miss the point if he allows this information to be superseded by the superior historical knowledge of our day.

The text of *The Prince* has many variations arising from the facts that no original manuscript in Machiavelli's hand exists and that the work was not published in his lifetime under his supervision. Those who want to examine the philological scholarship seeking to establish an authoritative text should begin with the article of Quaglio listed in the bibliography. I have followed the text of Casella for the most part, adopting some variants where they seemed appropriate.

Such are the principles of this translation. I have profited from other translations, especially from that of Leo Paul S. de Alvarez. If the reader thinks my translation a bad one, let him try his own; if he thinks it good, let him learn Italian.

Chronology

1469   (May 3) NM born in Florence, son of Bernardo
        (October) Ferdinand, heir to Aragon, marries Isabella, heir to
        Castille
        (December) death of Piero de' Medici
1476   Niccolò at school
1478   Pazzi conspiracy in which Giuliano is killed in the cathedral
        and Lorenzo escapes, becoming the dominant figure in
        Florence
1482   Savonarola begins to preach in Florence
1483   death of Louis XI, king of France; Charles VIII succeeds at
        age 13
1491   marriage of Charles VIII with Anne of Brittany, effectively
        the unification of France
1492   taking of Granada by Ferdinand, effectively the unification of
        Spain
        (April 8) death of Lorenzo de' Medici (Lorenzo the Magnifi-
        cent), succeeded by his son Piero
        (August 11) Rodrigo Borja (Borgia) becomes pope; takes
        name of Alexander VI
1494   King Charles VIII of France invades Italy; the Medici ex-
        pelled from Florence; Savonarola gains authority there
1498   (April 8) death of Charles VIII, succeeded by Louis XII
        (May 23) Savonarola excommunicated and burned at the
        stake in the Piazza della Signoria in Florence
        NM put at head of Second Chancery of the Florentine Re-
        public, also Secretary to the Ten of War
        Cesare Borgia (son of Pope Alexander VI) made Duke of the
        Valentinois (Duke Valentino)
1499   mission of NM to Forlì
        (August–October) Army of Louis XII enters Italy, captures
        Milan
        (September 28) Paolo Vitelli, condottiere for Florence, led to
        Florence and beheaded
1500   (February 5) Ludovico Sforza (il Moro) retakes Milan from
        the French
        (April 10) French retake Milan and imprison Ludovico
        (June and July) NM at the Florentine siege of Pisa

(August 7–December) NM on mission to court of France, meeting Louis XII and Georges d'Amboise, Cardinal of Rouen

1501   (February 2) NM at Pistoia
Cesare Borgia named Duke of Romagna by his father
(August 18) NM in Siena with its lord, Pandolfo Petrucci
NM marries Marietta Corsini

1502   NM on missions to Cesare Borgia in Romagna
(December 31) Cesare has Vitellozzo (brother of Paolo Vitelli) and Oliverotto strangled at Sinigaglia

1503   (August 18) death of Alexander VI
(October 23–December 18) NM on mission to Rome
(November 1) Julius II created pope; he then forces Cesare Borgia to give over his conquests to the Church

1504   NM again sent to France; writes the first *Decennale,* a poem on events in Italy since 1494

1505   NM sent on missions to Perugia, Mantua, Siena; begins on plan for militia in Florence

1506   NM sent to Julius II, follows him in his expedition to the Romagna
(September 13) NM with Julius II as he enters Perugia, ruled by Baglioni

1507   NM on mission to court of Emperor Maximilian; Cesare Borgia dies

1508   (February) NM at the siege of Pisa

1509   NM again in France and Siena

1511   (October 4) Pope Julius forms Holy League to resist France

1512   (April 11) Battle of Ravenna won by France, but its general, Gaston de Foix, killed
(August 31) Piero Soderini overthrown; Florentine republic ends; Medici family returns to power
(November 7) NM expelled from his position

1513   (February 19) NM suspected of conspiracy against the Medici; he is arrested, imprisoned, and tortured
(February 21) death of Pope Julius II; succeeded by Giovanni de' Medici, Pope Leo X
(March 13) NM freed; exiled to his country home in Sant'Andrea in Percussina, south of Florence
(December 10) NM writes to his friend Francesco Vettori

that he has completed *The Prince;* he also begins writing his *Discourses on Livy*

1515 (January 1) death of Louis XII, Francis I succeeds

1516 (January 23) death of Ferdinand of Aragon; Charles V succeeds

1517 NM writes the *Golden Ass,* an unfinished poem; frequents the Orti Oricellari, gardens owned by his friend Cosimo Rucellai, for philosophical discussions

1518 NM writes his comedy the *Mandragola*

1520 NM writes *The Life of Castruccio Castracani;* is commissioned by Cardinal Giulio de' Medici to write the *Florentine Histories*

1521 publication of NM's *The Art of War*

1522 Cardinal Giulio de' Medici succeeds to papacy as Clement VII

1525 NM in Rome presents the *Florentine Histories* to Clement VII

1527 Rome sacked by Emperor Charles V
(June 21) death of Machiavelli; buried in the Church of Santa Croce in Florence

1531 first edition published of NM's *Discourses on Livy,* with papal privilege

1532 first edition published of NM's *The Prince,* also with papal privilege

Italy in
Machiavelli's Time

0 50 100 150 200 kms

0   50   100 150 miles

THE
PRINCE

Dedicatory Letter

Niccolò Machiavelli to the Magnificent Lorenzo de' Medici:

It is customary most of the time for those who desire to acquire favor[1] with a Prince to come to meet him with things that they care most for among their own or with things that they see please him most. Thus, one sees them[2] many times being presented with horses, arms, cloth of gold, precious stones and similar ornaments worthy of their greatness. Thus, since I desire to offer myself to your Magnificence[3] with some testimony of my homage[4] to you, I have found nothing in my belongings that I care so much for and esteem so greatly as the knowledge of the actions of great men, learned by me from long experience with modern things and a continuous reading of ancient ones. Having thought out and examined these things with great diligence for a long time, and now reduced them to one small volume, I send it to your Magnificence.

And although I judge this work undeserving of your presence, yet I have much confidence that through your humanity it may be accepted, considering that no greater gift could be made by me than to give you the capacity to be able to understand in a very short time all that I have learned

---

1. lit.: acquire grace. "Acquire" is an economic term that NM often uses to refer to noneconomic gain, especially conquest—here, to the favor or grace that would seem to be in the gift of a prince.

2. NM switches from a singular to the plural, a device he uses frequently.

3. Lorenzo de' Medici (1492–1519), grandson of Lorenzo the Magnificent (1449–92); he became duke of Urbino in 1516. NM had at first intended to dedicate *The Prince* to Giuliano de' Medici, son of Lorenzo the Magnificent and duke of Nemours, who died in 1516. See NM's letter to Vettori of December 10, 1513, printed in the Appendix.

4. *servitù*, a feudal term of submission elsewhere to be translated as "servitude."

and understood in so many years and with so many hardships and dangers for myself. I have not ornamented this work, nor filled it with fulsome phrases nor with pompous and magnificent words, nor with any blandishment or superfluous ornament whatever, with which it is customary for many to describe and adorn their things. For I wanted it either not to be honored for anything or to please solely for the variety of the matter and the gravity of the subject. Nor do I want it to be reputed presumption if a man from a low and mean state dares to discuss and give rules for the governments of princes. For just as those who sketch landscapes place themselves down in the plain to consider the nature of mountains and high places and to consider the nature of low places place themselves high atop mountains, similarly, to know well the nature of peoples one needs to be prince, and to know well the nature of princes one needs to be of the people.

Therefore, your Magnificence, take this small gift in the spirit[5] with which I send it. If your Magnificence considers and reads it diligently, you will learn from it my extreme desire that you arrive at the greatness that fortune and your other qualities promise you. And if your Magnificence will at some time turn your eyes from the summit of your height to these low places, you will learn how undeservedly I endure a great and continuous malignity of fortune.

5. *animo* refers to the "spirit" with which human beings defend themselves, never to a capacity for self-detachment (*anima*, "soul," does not occur in *The Prince*). It can also mean "mind" in the sense of "intent," but not in the sense of "intellect."

OF PRINCIPALITIES

❧ I ❧

How Many Are the Kinds of Principalities and in What Modes They Are Acquired[1]

All states,[2] all dominions that have held and do hold empire over men have been and are either republics or principalities. The principalities are either hereditary, in which the bloodline[3] of their lord has been their prince for a long time, or they are new. The new ones are either altogether new, as was Milan to Francesco Sforza,[4] or they are like members added to the hereditary state of the prince who acquires them, as is the kingdom of Naples to the king of Spain.[5]

---

1. Chapter headings of *The Prince* are in Latin, the language of traditional learning and of the Church.

2. *stato* means both status (see the Dedicatory Letter) and state, as today, but the meanings are more closely connected; *stato* is the status of a person or a group while dominating someone else. Although NM sometimes speaks of "the state," he always means someone's state and does not refer to an impersonal state.

3. lit.: blood.

4. Francesco Sforza (1401–66), the mercenary captain, acquired Milan by betraying and overthrowing the Ambrosian Republic of Milan in 1450. In 1447 he had laid claim to Milan with a certain respect for its previous bloodline, through his marriage to Bianca, daughter of Filippo Maria Visconti, then duke of Milan. See NM's account in *Florentine Histories*, V 13, VI 13, 17–22.

5. Ferdinand the Catholic, after agreeing by treaty in 1500 to share the kingdom of Naples with Louis XII of France, drove out the French in 1504 and joined that kingdom to Spain.

Dominions so acquired are either accustomed to living under a prince or used to being free; and they are acquired either with the arms of others or with one's own, either by fortune or by virtue.[6]

6. In this translation *virtù* is consistently rendered "virtue."

❧ II ☙

Of Hereditary Principalities

I shall leave out reasoning on republics because I have reasoned on them at length another time.[1] I shall address myself only to the principality, and shall proceed by weaving together the threads mentioned above; and I shall debate how these principalities may be governed and maintained.

I say, then, that in hereditary states accustomed to the bloodline[2] of their prince the difficulties in maintaining them are much less than in new states because it is enough only not to depart from the order of his ancestors, and then to temporize in the face of accidents. In this way, if such a prince is of ordinary industry,[3] he will always main-

1. A reference to NM's other chief work, the *Discourses on Livy,* in which he reasons with the use of materials from Livy's history of the Roman republic, among other sources. NM does in fact discuss republics in *The Prince* (e.g., on "the Romans," Chapter 3 below), but not "at length."
2. lit.: blood.
3. *industria* for NM means diligence combined with skill or adroitness which is not necessarily visible.

tain himself in his state unless there is an extraordinary and excessive force which deprives him of it; and should he be deprived of it, if any mishap whatever befalls the occupier, he reacquires it.

We have in Italy, for example, the duke of Ferrara, who, for no other cause than that his line was ancient in that dominion, did not succumb to the attacks of the Venetians in '84, nor to those of Pope Julius in '10.[4] For the natural prince has less cause and less necessity to offend;[5] hence it is fitting that he be more loved. And if extraordinary vices do not make him hated, it is reasonable that he will naturally have the good will of his own. In the antiquity and continuity of the dominion the memories and causes of innovations are eliminated; for one change always leaves a dentation[6] for the building of another.

4. NM speaks of two dukes of Ferrara as if they were one: Ercole d'Este (1431–1505) and his son Alfonso d'Este (1476–1534). Ercole was defeated by the Venetians in 1484, and Alfonso was temporarily deprived of his principality by Pope Julius in 1510.

5. *Offendere* is not merely to slight, but to harm so as to cause offense.

6. A dentation is a toothed wall left on the side of a building so that another building may be attached to it. NM's metaphor compares the hereditary, or "natural," principality to a row of houses continually added to but never finished and, as it were, not begun from the beginning.

❧ III ☙

Of Mixed Principalities

But the difficulties reside in the new principality. First, if it is not altogether new but like an added member (so that taken as a whole it can be called almost mixed), its instability arises in the first place from a natural difficulty that exists in all new principalities. This is[1] that men willingly change their lords in the belief that they will fare better: this belief makes them take up arms against him, in which they are deceived because they see later by experience that they have done worse. That follows from another natural and ordinary necessity which requires that one must always offend those over whom he becomes a new prince, both with men-at-arms and with infinite other injuries that the new acquisition brings in its wake. So you have as enemies all those whom you have offended in seizing that principality, and you cannot keep as friends those who have put you there because you cannot satisfy them in the mode they had presumed and because you cannot use strong medicines against them, since you are obligated to them. For even though one may have the strongest of armies, he always needs the support of the inhabitants of a province[2] in order to enter it. Through these causes Louis XII of France quickly occupied Milan, and quickly lost it; and Ludovico's own forces were enough to take it from him the first time.[3] For those people which had opened the gates to him, finding themselves deceived in their opinion and in that future good they had presumed for themselves, were unable to tolerate the vexations of the new prince.

It is indeed true that when countries that have rebelled are later acquired for the second time, they are lost with more difficulty, because the lord, seizing the opportunity offered by the rebellion, is less hesitant[4] to secure himself by

1. lit.: these are.
2. "Province" refers to a country or region that may be larger or smaller than a "state."
3. Ludovico Sforza, il Moro, was duke of Milan from 1494 until Milan was seized from him in September 1499 by Louis XII. He recaptured Milan in February 1500 but was betrayed by his Swiss mercenaries at Novara, when the French acquired it in April "for the second time." The French then lost Milan in 1512 after the battle of Ravenna to the Holy League led by Pope Julius II, "the whole world."
4. *respettivo* is also translated as "cautious"; see especially Chapter 25.

punishing offenders, exposing suspects, and providing for himself in the weakest spots. So it was that, if one Duke Ludovico stirring up a commotion at the borders was enough to make France lose Milan the first time, to make him then lose it the second time, the whole world had to be against him, and his armies eliminated or chased from Italy: this arises from the causes given above. Nonetheless, both the first and the second times it was taken from him.

The universal causes of the first have been discussed; it remains now to say what were the causes of the second, and to see what remedies there were to him, which someone in his situation could use so as to maintain himself better in his acquisition than France did. Now I say, that such states which, when acquired, are added to an ancient state of him who acquires them, are either of the same province and same language, or not. When they are, they may be held with great ease, especially if they are not used to living free; and to possess them securely it is enough to have eliminated the line of the prince whose dominions they were. For when their old conditions are maintained for them in other things and there is no disparity of customs, men live quietly—as it may be seen that Burgundy, Brittany, Gascony, and Normandy, which have been with France for so long a time, have done;[5] and although there may be some disparity of language, nonetheless the customs are similar, and they can easily bear with one another. And whoever acquires them, if he wants to hold them, must have two concerns: one, that the bloodline of their ancient prince be eliminated; the other, not to alter either their laws or their taxes: so that in a very short time it becomes one whole body with their ancient principality.

But when one acquires states in a province disparate in language, customs, and orders, here are the difficulties, and here one needs to have great fortune and great industry to

5. Burgundy since 1477, Brittany 1491, Gascony 1453, and Normandy 1204.

hold them, and one of the greatest and quickest remedies would be for whoever acquires it to go there to live in person. This would make that possession more secure and more lasting, as the Turk has done in Greece. Despite all the other orders observed by him so as to hold that state, if he had not gone there to live, it would not have been possible for him to hold it. For if you stay there, disorders may be seen as they arise, and you can soon remedy them; if you are not there, disorders become understood when they are great and there is no longer a remedy. Besides this, the province is not despoiled by your officials; the subjects are satisfied with ready access to the prince, so that they have more cause to love him if they want to be good and, if they want to be otherwise, more cause to fear him. Whatever outsider might want to attack that state has more hesitation in doing so; hence, when one lives in it, one can lose it with the greatest difficulty.

The other, better remedy is to send colonies that are, as it were, fetters of that state, to one or two places, because it is necessary either to do this or to hold them with many men-at-arms and infantry. One does not spend much on colonies, and without expense of one's own, or with little, one may send them and hold them; and one offends only those from whom one takes fields and houses in order to give them to new inhabitants—who are a very small part of that state. And those whom he offends, since they remain dispersed and poor, can never harm him, while all the others remain on the one hand unhurt, and for this they should be quiet; on the other, they are afraid to err from fear that what happened to the despoiled might happen to them. I conclude that such colonies are not costly, are more faithful, and less offensive; and those who are offended can do no harm, since they are poor and dispersed as was said. For this has to be noted: that men should either be caressed or eliminated, because they avenge themselves for slight offenses but cannot do so for grave ones; so the offense one does to a man should be such that one does not fear revenge for it. But when one holds a state with men-at-arms in place of colonies, one spends much more since one has to consume all the income of that state in guarding it. So the acquisition turns to loss, and one offends much more because one harms the whole state as one's army moves around for lodgings. Everyone feels this hardship, and each becomes one's enemy: and these are enemies that can harm one since they remain, though defeated, in their homes. From every side, therefore, keeping guard in this way is as useless as keeping guard by means of colonies is useful.

Whoever is in a province that is disparate, as was said, should also make himself head and defender of the neighboring lesser powers, and contrive to weaken the powerful in that province and to take care that through some accident a foreigner as powerful as he does not enter there. And it will always turn out that a foreigner will be brought in by those in the province who are malcontent either because of too much ambition or out of fear, as once the Aetolians were seen to bring the Romans into Greece; and in every other province they entered, they were brought in by its inhabitants. And the order of things is such that as soon as a powerful foreigner enters a province, all those in it who are less powerful adhere to him, moved by the envy they have against whoever has held power over them. So with respect to these lesser powers, he has no trouble in gaining them, because all together they quickly and willingly make one mass with the state that he has acquired there. He has only to worry that these lesser powers may get too much force and too much authority; and with his forces and their support he can easily put down those who are powerful, so as to remain arbiter of that province in everything. And whoever does not conduct this policy well will soon lose what he has acquired, and while he holds it, will have infinite difficulties and vexations within it.

The Romans observed these policies well in the

provinces they took. They sent out colonies, indulged the lesser powers without increasing their power, put down the powerful, and did not allow foreign powers to gain reputation there. And I want the province of Greece alone to suffice as an example. The Achaeans and the Aetolians were indulged by the Romans; the kingdom of the Macedonians was brought down and Antiochus was chased out. Nor did the merits of the Achaeans or those of the Aetolians make the Romans permit them to increase any state of theirs; nor did the persuasions of Philip ever induce them to be his friends without putting him down; nor could the power of Antiochus make them consent to his holding any state in that province. For the Romans did in these cases what all wise princes should do: they not only have to have regard for present troubles[6] but also for future ones, and they have to avoid these with all their industry because, when one foresees from afar, one can easily find a remedy for them but when you wait until they come close to you, the medicine is not in time because the disease has become incurable. And it happens with this as the physicians say of consumption, that in the beginning of the illness it is easy to cure and difficult to recognize, but in the progress of time, when it has not been recognized and treated in the beginning, it becomes easy to recognize and difficult to cure. So it happens in affairs of state, because when one recognizes from afar the evils that arise in a state (which is not given but to one who is prudent), they are soon healed; but when they are left to grow because they were not recognized, to the point that everyone recognizes them, there is no longer any remedy for them.

Thus, the Romans, seeing inconveniences from afar, always found remedies for them and never allowed them to continue so as to escape a war, because they knew that war may not be avoided but is deferred to the advantage of

6. lit.: scandals.

others. So they decided to make war with Philip and Antiochus in Greece in order not to have to do so in Italy; and they could have avoided both one and the other for a time, but they did not want to. Nor did that saying ever please them which is every day in the mouths of the wise men of our times—to enjoy the benefit of time—but rather, they enjoyed the benefit of their virtue and prudence. For time sweeps everything before it and can bring with it good as well as evil and evil as well as good.

But let us return to France and examine whether he has done any of the things spoken of. I will speak of Louis and not of Charles,[7] as the steps of the former, because he held his possession in Italy longer, may be seen better. And you[8] will see that he did the contrary of the things that should be done to hold a state in a disparate province.

King Louis was brought into Italy by the ambition of the Venetians, who wanted to gain half the state of Lombardy for themselves by his coming. I do not want to blame the course adopted by the king; for since he wanted to begin by gaining a foothold in Italy, and having no friends in this province, indeed, having all doors closed to him because of the conduct of King Charles, he was forced to take whatever friendships he could get. And having firmly adopted this course he would have succeeded if in managing other things he had not made some error. Thus, when he had acquired Lombardy, the king regained quickly the reputation that Charles had taken from him: Genoa yielded, and the Florentines became his friends; the marquis of Mantua, duke of Ferrara, Bentivoglio, Madonna of Forlì, the lords of Faenza, of Pesaro, of Rimini, of Camerino, of Piombino, the Luccans, Pisans, and Sienese—everyone came to meet him so as to become his friend. And then the Venetians

7. Of Louis XII, not of Charles VIII; the latter's invasion of Italy in September 1494 lasted only until October 1495.
8. The formal or plural you.

could consider the temerity of the course they had adopted: to acquire two lands in Lombardy they made the king lord of two-thirds[9] of Italy.

One may now consider with how little difficulty the king could have maintained his reputation in Italy if he had observed the rules written above and had held secure and defended all those friends of his, who, because they were a great number, weak, and fearful—some of the Church, some of the Venetians—were always under a necessity to stay with him; and by their means he could always have secured himself easily against whoever remained great among us. But no sooner was he in Milan than he did the contrary by giving aid to Pope Alexander so that the pope might seize the Romagna. Nor did he notice that with this decision he was weakening himself, stripping himself of his friends and those who had jumped into his lap, while making the Church great by adding so much temporal greatness to the spiritual one that gives it so much authority. And having made the first error, he was compelled to continue, so that to put an end to the ambition of Alexander, and to prevent his becoming lord of Tuscany, he was compelled to come into Italy. It was not enough for him to have made the Church great and to have stripped himself of his friends, but because he wanted the kingdom of Naples, he divided it with the king of Spain. Whereas at first he was the arbiter of Italy, he brought in a companion so that the ambitious ones in that province and those malcontent with him had somewhere to turn; and whereas he could have left in that kingdom[10] a king who was his pensioner, he threw him out so as to bring in one who could expel him.

And truly it is a very natural and ordinary thing to desire to acquire, and always, when men do it who can, they will be praised or not blamed; but when they cannot,

9. Some manuscripts say one-third.
10. The kingdom of Naples, which had been held by Frederick of Aragon.

and wish to do it anyway, here lie the error and the blame. Thus, if France could have attacked Naples with his own forces, he should have done so; if he could not, he should not have divided Naples. And if the division of Lombardy he made with the Venetians deserves excuse because with it France gained a foothold in Italy, this other one deserves blame because it was not excused by that necessity.

So then Louis had made these five errors: he had eliminated the lesser powers; increased the power of a power in Italy; brought in a very powerful foreigner; did not come to live there; did not put colonies there. Yet if he had lived, these errors could not have hurt him if he had not made a sixth: depriving the Venetians of their state. For if he had not made the Church great or brought Spain into Italy, it would indeed have been reasonable and necessary to put down the Venetians. But when he had adopted these courses first, he should never have consented to their ruin, for while they were powerful they would always have kept others away from a campaign in Lombardy, whether it was because the Venetians would not have consented to them unless they themselves were to become its lords, or because the others would not have wanted to take Lombardy from France in order to give it to the Venetians, and they would not have had the spirit to go and attack both of them. And if someone should say: King Louis ceded Romagna to Alexander and the Kingdom[11] to Spain to avoid a war, I reply with the reasons given above: that a disorder should never be allowed to continue so as to avoid a war, because that is not to avoid it but to defer it to your disadvantage. And if some others should cite the faith that the king had pledged to the pope, to undertake that enterprise for him in return for dissolving his marriage and for the hat of Rouen,[12] I reply with what I will say below on the faith of

11. The kingdom of Naples, often styled "the Kingdom."

12. Louis XII had obtained from the pope an annulment of his marriage to Jeanne de Valois and a cardinalate (with hat) for his minister, Georges d' Amboise, bishop of Rouen.

princes and how it should be observed.[13] Thus, King Louis lost Lombardy for not having observed any of the conditions observed by others who have taken provinces and wished to hold them. Nor is this any miracle, but very ordinary and reasonable. And I spoke of this matter at Nantes with Rouen[14] when Valentino (for so Cesare Borgia, son of Pope Alexander, was called by the people) was occupying Romagna. For when the cardinal of Rouen said to me that the Italians do not understand war, I replied to him that the French do not understand the state, because if they understood they would not have let the Church come to such greatness. And it may be seen from experience that the greatness in Italy of the Church and of Spain has been caused by France, and France's ruin caused by them. From this one may draw a general rule that never or rarely fails: whoever is the cause of someone's becoming powerful is ruined; for that power has been caused by him either with industry or with force, and both the one and the other of these two are suspect to whoever has become powerful.

13. See Chapter 18 below.
14. During NM's first diplomatic mission to France; see his letter of November 21, 1500.

❧ IV ❧

Why the Kingdom of Darius Which Alexander Seized Did Not Rebel from His Successors after Alexander's Death

The difficulties that are involved in holding a state newly acquired having been considered, one might marvel at how it happened that Alexander the Great became lord of Asia in a few years, and just after he had seized it, died—from which it appeared reasonable that all that state would rebel—nonetheless the successors of Alexander maintained it and had no other difficulty in holding it than that which arose among themselves out of their own ambition.[1] I reply that principalities of which memory remains have been governed in two diverse modes: either by one prince, and all the others servants who as ministers help govern the kingdom by his favor and appointment; or by a prince and by barons who hold that rank not by favor of the lord but by antiquity of bloodline. Such barons have their own states and subjects who recognize them as lords and hold them in natural affection. States that are governed by one prince and his servants hold their prince in greater authority because in all his province there is no one recognized as superior but himself; and if they obey someone else, they do so as a minister and official, and do not bear him any particular love.

In our times the examples of these two diverse kinds of government are the Turk and the king of France. The whole monarchy of the Turk is governed by one lord; the others are his servants. Dividing his kingdom into sanjaks,[2] he sends different administrators to them, and he changes and varies them as he likes. But the king of France is placed in the midst of an ancient multitude of lords, acknowledged in that state by their subjects and loved by them: they have their privileges, and the king cannot take them away without danger to himself. Thus, whoever considers the one and the other of these states will find difficulty in acquiring the state of the Turk, but should it be conquered, great ease in holding it. So inversely, you[3] will find in some respects

1. NM apparently refers to Alexander's rapid occupation of "Asia" in seven years, from 334 to 327 B.C., and its division among seven generals, eventually into eleven kingdoms, after his death.
2. Administrative units.
3. The formal or plural you.

more ease in seizing the state of France, but great difficulty in holding it.

The causes of the difficulties in being able to seize the kingdom of the Turk are that one cannot be called in by the princes in that kingdom, and that one cannot hope to facilitate the enterprise through the rebellion of those around him. This arises from the reasons given above, for, since all are slaves and bound by obligation, they can be corrupted with much difficulty, and even if they are corrupted, one can hope but for little use from it, as they cannot bring their peoples with them, for the reasons indicated. Hence, whoever attacks the Turk must necessarily assume that he will find him entirely united, and he had better put his hope more in his own forces than in the disorders of others. But once the Turk has been overcome and defeated in the field in such a way that he cannot rally his armies, one has only to fear the bloodline of the prince. If this is eliminated, there remains no one whom one would have to fear, since others do not have credit with the people; and just as the victor could put no hope in them before his victory, so he should not fear them after it.

The contrary occurs with kingdoms governed like France, because you can easily enter there, having won over to yourself some baron of the kingdom; for malcontents and those who desire to innovate are always to be found. For the reasons given, they can open the way for you into that state and facilitate victory for you. Then your wish to maintain that victory for yourself brings in its wake infinite difficulties both from those who have helped you and from those you have oppressed. Nor is it enough for you to eliminate the bloodline of the prince, because lords remain there who put themselves at the head of new changes; and since you can neither content them nor eliminate them, you lose that state whenever their opportunity comes.

Now, if you[4] consider what was the nature of Da-

4. The formal or plural you.

rius's[5] government, you[6] will find it similar to the kingdom of the Turk. Therefore, for Alexander it was necessary first to make an all-out attack on him and drive him from the field; after this victory, with Darius dead, that state remained secure for Alexander for the reasons discussed above. And if his successors had been united, they could have enjoyed it at leisure, nor did any tumults occur in that kingdom besides those they themselves incited. But it is impossible to possess states ordered like France with such quiet. Hence arose the frequent rebellions in Spain, France,[7] and Greece against the Romans, because of the numerous principalities that existed in those states. As long as their memory lasted, the Romans were always uncertain of their possession, but when their memory was eliminated with the power and long duration of the empire, the Romans became secure possessors of them. And the Romans possessed them even though, when they later fought among themselves, each took for himself a part of those provinces in accordance with the authority he had got within it; and the provinces, because the bloodline of their former lords was eliminated, acknowledged no one but the Romans. Having considered all these things, therefore, no one will marvel at the ease with which Alexander held the state of Asia and at the difficulties others such as Pyrrhus[8] and many more like him had in keeping their acquisitions. This has come not from much or little virtue in the victor but from the disparity in the subject.

5. Darius III (380–330 B.C.) was the king of Persia who lost his empire to Alexander the Great.

6. The formal or plural you.

7. NM was pleased to call ancient Gaul by its modern name; see *Discourses on Livy* II 4.

8. Pyrrhus (319–272 B.C.), king of Epirus, captured Sicily and quickly lost it.

How Cities or Principalities Which Lived by Their Own Laws before They Were Occupied Should Be Administered

When those states that are acquired, as has been said, are accustomed to living by their own laws and in liberty, there are three modes for those who want to hold them: first, ruin them; second, go there to live personally; third, let them live by their laws, taking tribute from them and creating within them an oligarchical state which keeps them friendly to you. For since such a state has been created by that prince, it knows it cannot stand without his friendship and power, and it has to do everything to maintain him. And a city used to living free may be held more easily by means of its own citizens than in any other mode, if one wants to preserve it.

As examples there are the Spartans and the Romans. The Spartans held Athens and Thebes by creating oligarchical states there; yet they lost them again.[1] The Romans, in order to hold Capua, Carthage, and Numantia, destroyed them and did not lose them.[2] They wanted to hold Greece much as the Spartans had held it, by making it free and leaving it its own laws. But they did not succeed; so they were compelled to destroy many cities in that province so as to hold it. For in truth there is no secure mode to possess them other than to ruin them. And whoever becomes pa-

---

1. In Athens the regime of Thirty Tyrants was established by Spartan direction in 404 B.C., then overthrown in 403. In Thebes the victorious Spartans established an oligarchy in 382 B.C., which was overthrown by Pelopidas in 378.
2. Capua was destroyed by the Romans after its rebellion, in 211 B.C.; Carthage was destroyed in 146 B.C.; and Numantia in 133 B.C.

tron of a city accustomed to living free and does not destroy it, should expect to be destroyed by it; for it always has as a refuge in rebellion the name of liberty and its own ancient orders which are never forgotten either through length of time or because of benefits received. Whatever one does or provides for, unless the inhabitants are broken up or dispersed, they will not forget that name and those orders, and will immediately recur to them upon any accident as did Pisa after having been kept in servitude a hundred years by the Florentines.[3] But, when cities or provinces are used to living under a prince, and his bloodline is eliminated—since on the one hand they are used to obeying, and on the other they do not have the old prince—they will not agree to make one from among themselves and they do not know how to live free. So they are slower to take up arms, and a prince can gain them with greater ease and can secure himself against them. But in republics there is greater life, greater hatred, more desire for revenge; the memory of their ancient liberty does not and cannot let them rest, so that the most secure path is to eliminate them or live in them.

3. Pisa was acquired by Florence in 1405 and lost in 1494 because of the invasion of the king of France, Charles VIII.

❧ VI ❧

Of New Principalities That Are Acquired through One's Own Arms and Virtue

No one should marvel if, in speaking as I will do of principalities that are altogether new both in prince and in state,

I bring up the greatest examples. For since men almost always walk on paths beaten by others and proceed in their actions by imitation, unable either to stay on the paths of others altogether or to attain the virtue of those whom you imitate, a prudent man should always enter upon the paths beaten by great men, and imitate those who have been most excellent, so that if his own virtue does not reach that far, it is at least in the odor of it. He should do as prudent archers do when the place they plan to hit appears too distant, and knowing how far the strength[1] of their bow carries, they set their aim much higher than the place intended, not to reach such height with their arrow, but to be able with the aid of so high an aim to achieve their plan.

I say, then, that in altogether new principalities, where there is a new prince, one encounters more or less difficulty in maintaining them according to whether the one who acquires them is more or less virtuous. And because the result of becoming prince from private individual presupposes either virtue or fortune, it appears that one or the other of these two things relieves in part many difficulties; nonetheless, he who has relied less on fortune has maintained himself more. To have the prince compelled to come to live there in person, because he has no other states, makes it still easier. But, to come to those who have become princes by their own virtue and not by fortune, I say that the most excellent are Moses, Cyrus, Romulus, Theseus, and the like. And although one should not reason about Moses, as he was a mere executor of things that had been ordered for him by God, nonetheless he should be admired if only for that grace which made him deserving of speaking with God. But let us consider Cyrus and the others who have acquired or founded kingdoms: you[2] will find them all admirable; and if their particular actions and orders are consid-

1. lit.: virtue.
2. The formal or plural you.

ered, they will appear no different from those of Moses, who had so great a teacher. And as one examines their actions and lives, one does not see that they had anything else from fortune than the opportunity, which gave them the matter enabling them to introduce any form they pleased. Without that opportunity their virtue of spirit would have been eliminated, and without that virtue the opportunity would have come in vain.

It was necessary then for Moses to find the people of Israel in Egypt, enslaved and oppressed by the Egyptians, so that they would be disposed to follow him so as to get out of their servitude. It was fitting that Romulus not be received in Alba, that he should have been exposed at birth, if he was to become king of Rome and founder of that fatherland. Cyrus needed to find the Persians malcontent with the empire of the Medes, and the Medes soft and effeminate because of a long peace. Theseus could not have demonstrated his virtue if he had not found the Athenians dispersed. Such opportunities, therefore, made these men happy, and their excellent virtue enabled the opportunity to be recognized; hence their fatherlands were ennobled by it and became very happy.

Those like these men, who become princes by the paths of virtue, acquire their principality with difficulty but hold it with ease; and the difficulties they have in acquiring their principality arise in part from the new orders and modes that they are forced to introduce so as to found their state and their security. And it should be considered that nothing is more difficult to handle, more doubtful of success, nor more dangerous to manage, than to put oneself at the head of introducing new orders. For the introducer has all those who benefit from the old orders as enemies, and he has lukewarm defenders in all those who might benefit from the new orders. This lukewarmness arises partly from fear of adversaries who have the laws on their side and partly from the incredulity of men, who do not truly believe in new things unless they come to have a firm experience of them. Consequently, whenever those who are enemies have opportunity to attack, they do so with partisan zeal, and the others defend lukewarmly so that one is in peril along with them. It is however necessary, if one wants to discuss this aspect well, to examine whether these innovators stand by themselves or depend on others; that is, whether to carry out their deed they must beg[3] or indeed can use force. In the first case they always come to ill and never accomplish anything; but when they depend on their own and are able to use force, then it is that they are rarely in peril. From this it arises that all the armed prophets conquered and the unarmed ones were ruined. For, besides the things that have been said, the nature of peoples is variable; and it is easy to persuade them of something, but difficult to keep them in that persuasion. And thus things must be ordered in such a mode that when they no longer believe, one can make them believe by force. Moses, Cyrus, Theseus, and Romulus would not have been able to make their peoples observe their constitutions for long if they had been unarmed, as happened in our times to Brother Girolamo Savonarola. He was ruined in his new orders as soon as the multitude began not to believe in them, and he had no mode for holding firm those who had believed nor for making unbelievers believe.[4] Men such as these, therefore, find great difficulty in conducting their affairs; all their dangers are along the path, and they must overcome them with virtue. But once they have overcome them and they begin to be held in veneration, having eliminated those who had

3. Or pray.

4. Savonarola (1452–98) was a Dominican friar who came to Florence to preach in 1481, and succeeded in convincing the Florentines, who thought themselves "neither rude nor ignorant," that "he spoke with God." Cf. *Discourses on Livy* I 11, where NM praises this accomplishment and does not refer, as he does here, to Savonarola's terrible end by burning at the stake.

envied them for their quality, they remain powerful, secure, honored, and happy.

To such high examples I want to add a lesser example, but it will have some proportion with the others and I want it to suffice for all other similar cases: this is Hiero of Syracuse. From private individual he became prince of Syracuse, nor did he receive anything more from fortune than the opportunity. For when the Syracusans were oppressed, they chose him as their captain, and from there he proved worthy of being made their prince. And he was of such virtue, even in private fortune, that he who wrote of him said "that he lacked nothing of being a king except a kingdom."[5] Hiero eliminated the old military and organized a new one; he left his old friendships and made new ones; and when he had friendships and soldiers that were his own, he could build any building on top of such a foundation; so he went through a great deal of trouble to acquire, and little to maintain.

5. Possible sources: Polybius, I 8, 16; VII 8; Livy XXIV 4; Justin, XXIII 4; I Samuel 18: 8. Cf. the Dedicatory Letter to the *Discourses on Livy*.

❧ VII ☙

Of New Principalities That Are Acquired by Others' Arms and Fortune

Those who become princes from private individual solely by fortune become so with little trouble, but maintain themselves with much. They have no difficulty along the path because they fly there, but all the difficulties arise when they are in place. And such princes come to be when a state is given to someone either for money or by the favor of whoever gives it, as happened to many in Greece, in the cities of Ionia and of the Hellespont, where they were made princes by Darius so that they might hold on to those cities for his security and glory;[1] as also those emperors were made who from private individual attained the empire through corrupting the soldiers.[2] These persons rest simply on the will and fortune of whoever has given a state to them, which are two very inconstant and unstable things. They do not know how to hold and they cannot hold that rank: they do not know how, because if one is not a man of great ingenuity and virtue, it is not reasonable, that having always lived in private fortune, he should know how to command; they cannot hold that rank because they do not have forces that can be friendly and faithful to them. Then, too, states that come to be suddenly, like all other things in nature that are born and grow quickly, cannot have roots and branches, so that the first adverse weather[3] eliminates them—unless, indeed, as was said, those who have suddenly become princes have so much virtue that they know immediately how to prepare to keep what fortune has placed in their laps; and the foundations that others have laid before becoming princes they lay afterwards.

To both of the modes mentioned of becoming prince, by virtue or by fortune, I want to bring up two examples that have occurred in days within our memory; and these are Francesco Sforza and Cesare Borgia. Francesco became duke of Milan from private individual by proper means[4] and with a great virtue of his own; and that which he had acquired with a thousand pains he maintained with little trouble. On the other hand Cesare Borgia, called Duke

1. Darius I (521–486 B.C.), not Darius III of Chapter 4.
2. On the election of Roman emperors by soldiers, see Chapter 19.
3. Or time.
4. For this phrase see NM, *Discourses on Livy* I 41.

Valentino by the vulgar, acquired his state through the fortune of his father and lost it through the same, notwithstanding the fact that he made use of every deed and did all those things that should be done by a prudent and virtuous man to put his roots in the states that the arms and fortune of others had given him. For, as was said above, whoever does not lay his foundations at first might be able, with great virtue, to lay them later, although they might have to be laid with hardship for the architect and with danger to the building. Thus, if one considers all the steps of the duke, one will see that he had laid for himself great foundations for future power, which I do not judge superfluous to discuss; for I do not know what better teaching I could give to a new prince than the example of his actions. And if his orders did not bring profit to him, it was not his fault, because this arose from an extraordinary and extreme malignity of fortune.

Alexander VI had very many difficulties, both present and future, when he decided to make his son the duke great. First, he did not see the path to being able to make him lord of any state that was not a state of the Church; and when he decided to take that of the Church, he knew that the duke of Milan and the Venetians would not consent to it because Faenza and Rimini had for long been under the protection of the Venetians. Besides this, he saw that the arms of Italy, and especially the arms of anyone whom he might have been able to make use of, were in the hands of those who had to fear the greatness of the pope; and so he could not trust them, as they were all with the Orsini and the Colonna and their accomplices.[5] It was thus necessary to upset those orders and to bring disorder to their states so as to be able to make himself lord securely of part of them. This was easy for him, because he found that the Venetians, moved by other causes, were engaged in getting the French to come

5. The Orsini and Colonna were the two principal noble families of Rome which had long fought for control of Rome and the papacy.

back into Italy, which he not only did not oppose but made easier by the dissolution of the former marriage of King Louis. So the king came into Italy with the aid of the Venetians and the consent of Alexander, and he was no sooner in Milan than the pope got men from him for a campaign in Romagna, which was granted to him because of the reputation of the king. So after the duke had acquired Romagna and beaten down the Colonna, two things prevented him from maintaining that and going further ahead: one, that his arms did not appear to him to be faithful; the other, the will of France: that is, the Orsini arms of which he had availed himself might fail under him, and not only prevent him from acquiring but also take away what he had acquired; and the king might also do the same to him. He had a test of the Orsini when, after the capture of Faenza, he attacked Bologna and saw them go coolly to that attack; and regarding the king, the duke knew his mind when after he had taken the duchy of Urbino, he attacked Tuscany, and the king made him desist from that campaign. Hence the duke decided to depend no longer on the arms and fortune of others. And the first thing he did was to weaken the Orsini and Colonna parties in Rome. For he gained to himself all their adherents, who were gentlemen, by making them his gentlemen and by giving them large allowances; and he honored them, according to their qualities, with commands and with government posts, so that in a few months the partisan affections in their minds were eliminated, and all affection turned toward the duke. After this he waited for an opportunity to eliminate the heads of the Orsini, since he had dispersed those of the Colonna house. A good one came to him, and he used it better; for when the Orsini became aware, late, that the greatness of the duke and of the Church was ruin for them, they held a meeting at Magione, near Perugia.[6] From that arose rebellion in Urbino, tumults in

6. October 9, 1502.

Romagna, and infinite dangers for the duke, who overcame them all with the aid of the French. And when his reputation had been restored, he trusted neither France nor other external forces, and so as not to put them to the test, he turned to deceit. He knew so well how to dissimulate his intent that the Orsini themselves, through Signor Paolo, became reconciled with him. The duke did not fail to fulfill every kind of duty to secure Signor Paolo, giving him money, garments, and horses, so that their simplicity brought them into the duke's hands at Sinigaglia.[7] So, when these heads had been eliminated, and their partisans had been turned into his friends, the duke had laid very good foundations for his power, since he had all Romagna with the duchy of Urbino. He thought, especially, that he had acquired the friendship of Romagna, and that he had gained all those peoples to himself since they had begun to taste well-being.

And because this point is deserving of notice and of being imitated by others, I do not want to leave it out. Once the duke had taken over Romagna, he found it had been commanded by impotent lords who had been readier to despoil their subjects than to correct them, and had given their subjects matter for disunion, not for union. Since that province was quite full of robberies, quarrels, and every other kind of insolence, he judged it necessary to give it good government, if he wanted to reduce it to peace and obedience to a kingly arm. So he put there Messer Remirro de Orco, a cruel and ready man, to whom he gave the fullest power.[8] In a short time Remirro reduced it to peace and unity, with the very greatest reputation for himself. Then

7. See NM's narration of this event in "A Description of the Method Used by Duke Valentino in Killing Vitellozzo Vitelli, Oliverotto da Fermo, and Others," in Allan Gilbert, trans., *Chief Works of Machiavelli*, 3 vols. (Durham, N.C.: Duke University Press, 1965), 1:163–69.

8. power: *potestà*, not *potenzia;* the phrase recalls the papal claim of *plenitudo potestatis.*

the duke judged that such excessive authority was not necessary, because he feared that it might become hateful; and he set up a civil court in the middle of the province, with a most excellent president, where each city had its advocate. And because he knew that past rigors had generated some hatred for Remirro, to purge the spirits of that people and to gain them entirely to himself, he wished to show that if any cruelty had been committed, this had not come from him but from the harsh nature of his minister. And having seized this opportunity, he had him placed one morning in the piazza at Cesena in two pieces, with a piece of wood and a bloody knife beside him. The ferocity of this spectacle left the people at once satisfied and stupefied.

But let us return to where we left off. I say that when the duke found himself very powerful and secure in part against present dangers—since he had armed to suit himself and had in good part eliminated those arms which were near enough to have attacked[9] him—there remained for him, if he wanted to proceed with acquisition, to consider the king of France. For he knew that this would not be tolerated by the king, who had been late to perceive his error. And so he began to seek out new friendships and to vacillate with France in the expedition that the French were making toward the kingdom of Naples against the Spanish who were besieging Gaeta. His intent was to secure himself against them:[10] in which he would soon have succeeded, if Alexander had lived.

And these were his arrangements as to present things. But as to the future, he had to fear, first, that a new successor in the Church might not be friendly to him and might seek to take away what Alexander had given him. He thought he might secure himself against this in four modes: first, to eliminate the bloodlines of all those lords he had

9. lit.: offended.
10. assure himself of Spanish support, or against the French.

despoiled, so as to take that opportunity away from the pope; second, to win over to himself all the gentlemen in Rome, as was said, so as to be able to hold the pope in check with them; third, to make the College of Cardinals as much his as he could; fourth, to acquire so much empire before the pope died that he could resist a first attack[11] on his own. Of these four things he had accomplished three at the death of Alexander; the fourth he almost accomplished. For of the lords he had despoiled he killed as many as he could reach, and very few saved themselves; the Roman gentlemen had been won over to himself; in the College he had a very large party; and as to new acquisition, he had planned to become lord over Tuscany, he already possessed Perugia and Piombino, and he had taken Pisa under his protection. And, as soon as he did not have to pay regard to France (which he did not have to do any longer, since the French had already been stripped of the kingdom by the Spanish, so that each of them was forced of necessity to buy his friendship), he would have jumped on Pisa. After this, Lucca and Siena would have quickly yielded, in part through envy of the Florentines, in part through fear; the Florentines had no remedy. If he had succeeded in this (as he was succeeding the same year that Alexander died), he would have acquired such force and reputation that he would have stood by himself and would no longer have depended on the fortune and force of someone else, but on his own power[12] and virtue. But Alexander died five years after he[13] had begun to draw his sword. He left the duke with only the state of Romagna consolidated, with all the others in the air, between two very powerful enemy armies, and sick to death. And there was such ferocity and such virtue in the duke, and he knew so well how men have to be won over or lost, and

11. lit.: impetus.
12. *potenzia*.
13. Alexander or Cesare?

31

so sound were the foundations that he had laid in so little time, that if he had not had these armies on his back or if he had been healthy, he would have been equal to every difficulty. And that his foundations were good one may see: Romagna waited for him for more than a month; in Rome, though he was half-alive, he remained secure; and although the Baglioni, Vitelli, and Orsini came to Rome, none followed them against him; if he could not make pope whomever he wanted, at least it would not be someone he did not want. But if at the death of Alexander the duke had been healthy, everything would have been easy for him. And he told me, on the day that Julius II was created,[14] that he had thought about what might happen when his father was dying, and had found a remedy for everything, except that he never thought that at his death he himself would also be on the point of dying.

Thus, if I summed up all the actions of the duke, I would not know how to reproach him; on the contrary, it seems to me he should be put forward, as I have done, to be imitated by all those who have risen to empire through fortune and by the arms of others. For with his great spirit and high intention, he could not have conducted himself otherwise and the only things in the way of his plans were the brevity of Alexander's life and his own sickness. So whoever judges it necessary in his new principality to secure himself against enemies, to gain friends to himself, to conquer either by force or by fraud, to make himself loved and feared by the people, and followed and revered by the soldiers, to eliminate those who can or might offend[15] you, to renew old orders through new modes, to be severe and pleasant, magnanimous and liberal, to eliminate an unfaithful military, to create a new one, to maintain friend-

---

14. NM was in Rome at the time of the conclave that elected Julius II pope in October–December 1503.

15. *offendere* (here and below) is not merely to slight, but to harm so as to cause offense.

ships with kings and princes so that they must either benefit you with favor or be hesitant to offend you—can find no fresher examples than the actions of that man. One could only accuse him in the creation of Julius as pontiff, in which he made a bad choice; for, as was said, though he could not make a pope to suit himself, he could have kept anyone from being pope. And for the papacy he should never have consented to those cardinals whom he had offended or who, having become pope, would have to be afraid of him. For men offend either from fear or for hatred. Those whom he had offended were, among others, San Piero ad Vincula, Colonna, San Giorgio, Ascanio;[16] all the others, if they had become pope, would have had to fear him, except Rouen and the Spaniards, the latter because of kinship and obligation, the former for his power, because he was connected to the kingdom of France.[17] Therefore the duke, before everything else, should have created a Spaniard pope, and if he could not, should have consented to Rouen, and not San Piero ad Vincula. And whoever believes that among great personages new benefits will make old injuries be forgotten deceives himself.[18] So the duke erred in this choice and it was the cause of his ultimate ruin.

16. In this irreverent listing of cardinals, Giuliano della Rovere (who became Pope Julius II) is named by his church in Rome, San Pietro in Vincoli; Giovanni Colonna; Raffaelo Riario, named for San Giorgio; Ascanio Sforza.

17. Cardinal Georges d'Amboise, bishop of Rouen; see Chapter 3.

18. See NM, *Discourses on Livy* III 4.

❧ VIII ❧

Of Those Who Have Attained a
Principality through Crimes

But, because one becomes prince from private individual also by two modes which cannot be altogether attributed either to fortune or to virtue, I do not think they should be left out, although one of them can be reasoned about more amply where republics are treated.[1] These are when one ascends to a principality by some criminal and nefarious path or when a private citizen becomes prince of his fatherland by the support of his fellow citizens. And, to speak of the first mode, it will be shown with two examples, one ancient, the other modern, without entering otherwise into the merits of this issue, because I judge it sufficient, for whoever would find it necessary, to imitate them.

Agathocles the Sicilian[2] became king of Syracuse not only from private fortune but from a mean and abject one. Born of a potter, he always kept to a life of crime at every rank of his career; nonetheless, his crimes were accompanied with such virtue of spirit and body that when he turned to the military, he rose through its ranks to become praetor of Syracuse. After he was established in that rank, he decided to become prince and to hold with violence and without obligation to anyone else that which had been conceded to him by agreement. Having given intelligence of his plan to Hamilcar the Carthaginian, who was with his armies fighting in Sicily, one morning he assembled the people and Senate of Syracuse as if he had to decide things pertinent to the republic. At a signal he had ordered, he had all the senators and the richest of the people killed by his

1. See *Discourses on Livy*; note that NM does not say which of the two modes is reasoned about more amply "where republics are treated."
2. Agathocles lived from 361 to 289 B.C.; his tyranny began in 316.

soldiers. Once they were dead, he seized and held the principate[3] of that city without any civil controversy. And although he was defeated twice by the Carthaginians and in the end besieged, not only was he able to defend his city but also, leaving part of his men for defense against the siege, he attacked Africa with the others. In a short time he freed Syracuse from the siege and brought the Carthaginians to dire necessity; they were compelled of necessity to come to an agreement with him, to be content with the possession of Africa, and to leave Sicily to Agathocles. Thus, whoever might consider the actions and virtue of this man will see nothing or little that can be attributed to fortune. For as was said above, not through anyone's support but through the ranks of the military, which he had gained for himself with a thousand hardships and dangers, he came to the principate and afterwards he maintained it with many spirited and dangerous policies. Yet one cannot call it virtue to kill one's citizens, betray one's friends, to be without faith, without mercy, without religion; these modes can enable one to acquire empire, but not glory. For, if one considers the virtue of Agathocles in entering into and escaping from dangers, and the greatness of his spirit in enduring and overcoming adversities, one does not see why he has to be judged inferior to any most excellent captain. Nonetheless, his savage cruelty and inhumanity, together with his infinite crimes, do not permit him to be celebrated among the most excellent men. Thus, one cannot attribute to fortune or to virtue what he achieved without either.

In our times, during the reign of Alexander VI, Liverotto da Fermo,[4] having been left a fatherless child some years before, was brought up by a maternal uncle of his

3. Or principality; *principato* can mean the ruling or dominating office as well as the realm of domination.

4. Oliverotto Euffreducci da Fermo, who took power in Fermo on December 26, 1501, and a year later was strangled by order of Cesare Borgia at Sinigaglia.

called Giovanni Fogliani, and in the first years of his youth he was sent out to soldier under Paolo Vitelli[5] so that when he was versed in that discipline, he would attain an excellent rank in the military. Then when Paolo died, he fought under Vitellozzo, his brother, and in a very short time, since he was ingenious and dashing in person and spirit, he became the first man in his military. But as it appeared to him servile to be at the level of others, he thought that with the aid of certain citizens of Fermo to whom servitude was dearer than the liberty of their fatherland, and with support from the Vitelli, he would seize Fermo. And he wrote to Giovanni Fogliani that since he had been away from home a few years, he wanted to come to see him and his city, and in some part to acknowledge his patrimony; and because he had not troubled himself for anything but to acquire honor, he wanted to come in honorable fashion accompanied by a hundred horsemen of his friends and servants, so that his citizens might see that he had not spent the time in vain. He begged Giovanni to please order that he be received honorably by the inhabitants of Fermo, which would direct honor not only to him but to Giovanni himself, since Liverotto was his ward. Thereupon Giovanni did not fail in any proper duty to his nephew; and when Liverotto had been honorably received by the inhabitants of Fermo, he was lodged in Giovanni's house. There, after a few days had passed, and after he had waited to order secretly what was necessary for his future crime, he held a most solemn banquet to which he invited Giovanni Fogliani and all the first men of Fermo. And when the food and all other entertainments customary at such banquets had been enjoyed, Liverotto, with cunning,[6] opened certain grave discussions,[7] speaking of the

5. A famous condottiere, he was hired by the Florentines and then beheaded by them in 1499 for suspected treachery.
6. lit.: art.
7. lit.: reasonings.

greatness of Pope Alexander and of Cesare Borgia, his son, and of their undertakings. While Giovanni and the others were responding to these discussions, Liverotto at a stroke stood up, saying that these were things that should be spoken of in a more secret place; and he withdrew to a room into which Giovanni and all the other citizens came behind him. No sooner were they seated than soldiers came out of secret places and killed Giovanni and all the others. After this homicide, Liverotto mounted on horse, rode through the town and besieged the highest magistracy in the palace so that through fear they were compelled to obey him and to establish a government of which he was made prince. And since all those who could have hurt[8] him because they were malcontent were dead, he strengthened himself with new civil and military orders, so that in the period of one year that he held the principality, he was not only secure in the city of Fermo but had become fearsome to all his neighbors. And to overthrow him would have been as difficult as to overthrow Agathocles if he had not permitted himself to be deceived by Cesare Borgia when at Sinigaglia, as was said above, he took the Orsini and the Vitelli. There Liverotto too was taken, one year after the parricide he committed, and together with Vitellozzo, who had been his master in his virtues and crimes, he was strangled.

Someone could question how it happened that Agathocles and anyone like him, after infinite betrayals and cruelties, could live for a long time secure in his fatherland, defend himself against external enemies, and never be conspired against by his citizens, inasmuch as many others have not been able to maintain their states through cruelty even in peaceful times, not to mention uncertain times of war. I believe that this comes from cruelties badly used or well used. Those can be called well used (if it is permissible to speak well of evil) that are done at a stroke, out of the

<hr/>

8. lit.: offended.

necessity to secure oneself, and then are not persisted in but are turned to as much utility for the subjects as one can. Those cruelties are badly used which, though few in the beginning, rather grow with time than are eliminated. Those who observe the first mode can have some remedy for their state with God and with men, as had Agathocles; as for the others it is impossible for them to maintain themselves.

Hence it should be noted that in taking hold of a state, he who seizes it should review all the offenses necessary for him to commit, and do them all at a stroke, so as not to have to renew them every day and, by not renewing them, to secure men and gain them to himself with benefits. Whoever does otherwise, either through timidity or through bad counsel, is always under necessity to hold a knife in his hand; nor can one ever found himself on his subjects if, because of fresh and continued injuries, they cannot be secure against him. For injuries must be done all together, so that, being tasted less, they offend less; and benefits should be done little by little so that they may be tasted better.[9] And above all, a prince should live with his subjects so that no single accident whether bad or good has to make him change; for when necessities come in adverse times you will not be in time for evil, and the good that you do does not help you, because it is judged to be forced on you, and cannot bring you any gratitude.

9. See *Discourses on Livy* I 45.

ເຮ IX ຂ⌁

Of the Civil Principality

But, coming to the other policy, when a private citizen becomes prince of his fatherland, not through crime or

38

other intolerable violence but with the support of his fellow citizens (which one could call a civil principality; neither all virtue nor all fortune is necessary to attain it, but rather a fortunate astuteness)—I say that one ascends to this principality either with the support of the people or with the support of the great. For in every city these two diverse humors are found, which arises from this: that the people desire neither to be commanded nor oppressed by the great, and the great desire to command and oppress the people. From these two diverse appetites one of three effects occurs in cities: principality or liberty or license.

Principality is caused either by the people or by the great, according to which of these sides has the opportunity for it. For when the great see they cannot resist the people, they begin to give reputation to one of themselves, and they make him prince so that they can vent their appetite under his shadow. So too, the people, when they see they cannot resist the great, give reputation to one, and make him prince so as to be defended with his authority. He who comes to the principality with the aid of the great maintains himself with more difficulty than one who becomes prince with the aid of the people, because the former finds himself prince with many around him who appear to be his equals, and because of this he can neither command them nor manage them to suit himself. But he who arrives in the principality with popular support finds himself alone there, and around him has either no one or very few who are not ready to obey. Besides this, one cannot satisfy the great with decency and without injury to others, but one can satisfy the people; for the end of the people is more decent than that of the great, since the great want to oppress and the people want not to be oppressed. Furthermore, a prince can never secure himself against a hostile people, as they are too many; against the great, he can secure himself, as they are few. The worst that a prince can expect from a hostile people is to be abandoned by it; but from the great, when they are hostile, he must fear not only being abandoned but also that they may come against him, for since there is more foresight and more astuteness in the great, they always move in time to save themselves, and they seek rank from those they hope will win. Also, the prince always lives of necessity with the same people, but he can well do without the same great persons, since he can make and unmake them every day, and take away and give them reputation at his convenience.

And to better clarify this issue, I say that the great must be considered in two modes chiefly. Either they conduct themselves so that in their proceedings they are obligated in everything to your fortune, or not. Those who are obligated, and are not rapacious, must be honored and loved; those who are not obligated have to be examined in two modes. Either they do this out of pusillanimity and a natural defect of spirit; then you must make use especially of those who are of good counsel, because in prosperity they bring you honor and in adversity you do not have to fear them; but, when by art and for an ambitious cause, they are not obligated, it is a sign that they are thinking more for themselves than for you; and the prince must be on guard against them, and fear them as if they were open enemies, because in adversity they will always help ruin him.

Therefore, one who becomes prince through the support of the people should keep them friendly to him, which should be easy for him because they ask of him only that they not be oppressed. But one who becomes prince against the people with the support of the great must before everything else seek to gain the people to himself, which should be easy for him when he takes up its protection. And since men who receive good from someone from whom they believed they would receive evil are more obligated to their benefactor, the people immediately wish him well more than if he had been brought to the principality with their support. The prince can gain the people to himself in many modes, for which one cannot give certain rules because the modes vary according to circumstances,[1] and so they will be left out. I will conclude only that for a prince it is necessary to have the people friendly; otherwise he has no remedy in adversity.

Nabis, prince of the Spartans,[2] withstood a siege by all Greece and by one of Rome's most victorious armies, and defended his fatherland and his state against them: and when danger supervened it was enough for him to secure himself only against a few, which would not have been enough if he had had a hostile people. And let no one resist my opinion on this with that trite proverb, that whoever founds on the people founds on mud. For that is true when a private citizen lays his foundation on them, and allows himself to think that the people will liberate him if he is oppressed by enemies or by the magistrates (in this case one can often be deceived, like the Gracchi in Rome[3] and Messer Giorgio Scali in Florence).[4] But when a prince who founds on the people knows how to command and is a man full of heart, does not get frightened in adversity, does not fail to make other preparations, and with his spirit and his orders keeps the generality of people[5] inspired, he will never find himself deceived by them and he will see he has laid his foundations well.

These principalities customarily run into peril when

1. lit.: according to the subject.
2. NM considers Nabis a tyrant in *Discourses on Livy* I 10, 40; and in III 6 he tells how Nabis was assassinated despite his popular support. He ruled Sparta from 205 to 192 B.C.
3. The Gracchi brothers Tiberius and Gaius Sempronius were tribunes of the plebs but lost their lives to their enemies in the Senate, Tiberius in 133 and Gaius in 121 B.C.; see *Discourses on Livy* I 37.
4. A head of the Ciompi rebellion in Florence (1378), who ruled for three years thereafter and then was beheaded; see NM's *Florentine Histories* III 18, 20.
5. lit.: the universal. NM, in accord with the usage of his time, says "universal" in cases where we would expect "general," since apparently not everyone (not to mention everything) is meant.

they are about to ascend from a civil order to an absolute one. For these princes either command by themselves or by means of magistrates. In the latter case their position is weaker and more dangerous because they remain altogether at the will of those citizens who have been put in the magistracies, who, especially in adverse times, can take away his state with great ease either by turning against him or by not obeying him. And the prince does not have time in the midst of danger to seize absolute authority because the citizens and subjects, who are accustomed to receive commands from the magistrates, are not ready, in these emergencies, to obey his; he will always have, in uncertain times, a shortage of those one can trust. For such a prince cannot found himself on what he sees in quiet times, when citizens have need of the state, because then everyone runs, everyone promises, and each wants to die for him when death is at a distance; but in adverse times, when the state has need of citizens, then few of them are to be found. And this test is all the more dangerous since one cannot make it but once. And so a wise prince must think of a way by which his citizens, always and in every quality of time, have need of the state and of himself; and then they will always be faithful to him.

❧ X ❧

In What Mode the Forces of All Principalities Should Be Measured

In examining the qualities of these principalities one must admit another consideration; that is, whether a prince has enough of a state that he can rule by himself when he needs to, or whether he is always under the necessity of being defended by others. And, to better clarify this issue, I say that I judge those capable of ruling by themselves who can, by abundance of either men or money, put together an adequate army and fight a battle[1] against whoever comes to attack them; and I judge as well that those always have necessity of others who cannot appear in the field against an enemy, but are compelled of necessity to take refuge behind walls and to guard them. The first case has been discussed, and in what is to come we will say what is required for it. In the second case one can only exhort such princes to fortify and supply their own towns,[2] and to take no account of the countryside. And whoever has fortified his town well, and has managed the other governing of his subjects as was said above and will be said below, will be attacked always with great hesitation; for men are always hostile to undertakings where difficulties may be seen, and one can see it is not easy to attack one who has a strong town and is not hated by the people.

The cities of Germany[3] are very free, have little countryside, and obey the emperor when they want to; they do not fear either him or any other power around, because they are so well fortified that everyone thinks their capture would be toilsome and difficult. For all of them have suitable ditches and walls, and sufficient artillery; they always keep in their public stores enough to drink and to eat and to burn for a year. Besides this, so as to keep the plebs fed without loss to the public, they always keep in common supply enough to be able to give them work for a year in employments that are the nerve and the life of that city and of the industries from which the plebs is fed. They still hold

---

1. lit.: a just army and make a day; see NM, *Discourses on Livy* II 17.

2. lit.: land or earth.

3. NM discussed the German cities in *Discourses on Livy* I 55; II pr., 19; and also in two minor works, *Rapporto delle cose della Magna* and *Ritratto delle cose della Magna*.

military exercises in repute, and they have many institutions[4] to maintain them.

Thus a prince who has a strong city and does not make himself hated cannot be attacked; and if indeed there is someone who would attack him, he would have to retreat in shame, for worldly things are so variable that it is next to impossible for one to stand with his armies idle in a siege for a year. And someone might reply: if the people have their possessions outside, and see them burning, they will not have patience for this, and the long siege and their love[5] for their own will make them forget the prince. I respond that a powerful and spirited prince will always overcome all these difficulties, now by giving hope to his subjects that the evil will not last long, now by giving them fear of the enemy's cruelty, now by securing himself skillfully against those who appear to him too bold. Besides this, the enemy reasonably would burn and ruin the countryside on his arrival, at a time when men's spirits are still hot and willing for defense; and thus the prince should hesitate so much the less, because after several days, when spirits have cooled, the damage has already been done, the evil has been received, and there is no more remedy for it. At that time they come to unite with their prince so much the more, since it appears he has an obligation toward them, their houses having been burned and their possessions ruined in his defense. And the nature of men is to be obligated as much by benefits they give as by benefits they receive. Hence, if one considers all this well, it should not be difficult for a prudent prince to keep the spirits of his citizens firm in the siege, at first and later, provided he does not lack the wherewithal for life and for defense.

4. lit.: orders.
5. lit.: charity.

❧§ XI ❧

Of Ecclesiastical Principalities

—clergy

It remains now only to reason about ecclesiastical principalities. All difficulties regarding them come before they
are possessed, because they are acquired either by virtue or
by fortune and are maintained without the one or the other,
for they are sustained by orders that have grown old with
religion, which have been so powerful and of such a kind
that they keep their princes in the state however they proceed and live. These alone have states, and do not defend
them; they have subjects, and do not govern them; and the
states, though undefended, are not taken from them; the
subjects, though ungoverned, do not care, and they neither
think of becoming estranged from such princes nor can
they. Thus, only these principalities are secure and happy.
But as they subsist by superior causes,[1] to which the human mind does not reach, I will omit speaking of them; for
since they are exalted and maintained by God, it would
be the office of a presumptuous and foolhardy man to discourse on them. Nonetheless, if someone were to inquire of
me how it came about that the Church has come to such
greatness in temporal affairs despite the fact that, before
Alexander, the Italian powers, and not only those that are
called powers but every baron and lord, even the least, held
her in low esteem in temporal affairs—and now a king of
France trembles at her and she has been able to remove him
from Italy and to ruin the Venetians—though this is known,
it does not seem to me superfluous to recall a good part of it
to memory.

Before Charles, king of France, came into Italy,[2]
this province was under the power of the pope, the Vene-

1. Lisio and Bertelli read a singular "cause."
2. Charles VIII, in 1494.

tians, the king of Naples, the duke of Milan, and the Florentines. These powers had to have two principal concerns: one, that a foreigner not enter into Italy with arms; the other, that none of them enlarge his state. Those who concerned them the most were the pope and the Venetians. And to hold back the Venetians the union of all the others was needed, as in the defense of Ferrara; to hold down the pope they made use of the barons in Rome. Since these were divided into two factions, Orsini and Colonna, there was always cause for quarrel[3] between them; and standing with arms in hand under the eyes of the pontiff, they kept the pontificate weak and infirm. And although a spirited pope, like Sixtus,[4] sometimes rose up, still fortune or wisdom could never release him from these inconveniences. And the brevity of their lives was the cause of it; for in the ten years on the average that a pope lived, he would have trouble putting down one of the factions.[5] If, for instance, one pope had almost eliminated the Colonna, another one hostile to the Orsini rose up, which made the Colonna rise again, and there would not be time to eliminate the Orsini.

This brought the temporal forces of the pope to be held in low esteem in Italy. Then Alexander VI arose;[6] of all the pontiffs there have ever been he showed how far a pope could prevail with money and forces. With Duke Valentino as his instrument and with the invasion of the French as the opportunity, he did all the things I discussed above in the actions of the duke. And though his intent might not have been to make the Church great, but rather the duke, none-

3. lit.: scandal.
4. Sixtus IV (1414–84), pope from 1471 to 1484. NM said of him in *Florentine Histories* VII 22: "This pontiff was the first who began to show how much a pontiff could do and how many things previously called errors could be hidden under pontifical authority."
5. See NM, *Florentine Histories* I 23 (end).
6. NM omits Innocent VIII, pope from 1484 to 1492 between Sixtus IV and Alexander VI (who was pope from 1492 to 1503).

theless what he did redounded to the greatness of the Church. After his death, the duke being eliminated, the Church fell heir to his labors. Then came Pope Julius, and he found the Church great, since she had all Romagna, had eliminated the barons in Rome, and had annihilated those factions through the blows struck by Alexander; Julius found the path still open to a mode of accumulating money, never used before Alexander.[7] These things Julius not only continued but increased; and he thought about how to gain Bologna for himself, eliminate the Venetians, and expel the French from Italy. All these enterprises succeeded for him, and with all the more praise, inasmuch as he did everything for the increase of the Church and not of some private individual. He also kept the Orsini and Colonna parties within the same limits in which he found them; and although there might be some head among them ready to make a change, still two things restrained them: one, the greatness of the Church, which frightened them; the other, not having cardinals of their own, for they are the origin of the tumults among them. Nor will these parties ever be quiet as long as they have cardinals; for cardinals nourish parties, within Rome and without, and the barons are forced to defend them. Thus, from the ambition of prelates arise disorders and tumults among the barons. His Holiness Pope Leo,[8] then, has found this pontificate most powerful; one may hope that if the others made it great with arms, he, with his goodness and infinite other virtues, can make it very great and venerable.

7. Apparently the sale of ecclesiastical offices or indulgences.
8. Leo X, Giovanni de' Medici, son of Lorenzo de' Medici, pope from 1513 to 1521.

❧ XII ❧

How Many Kinds of Military There Are and Concerning Mercenary Soldiers

Having discoursed in particular on all the qualities of those principalities which at the beginning I proposed to reason about, having considered in some part the causes of their well-being and ill-being, and having shown the modes in which many have sought to acquire and hold them, it remains for me now to discourse generally on the offense and defense befitting each of those named. We have said above that it is necessary for a prince to have good foundations for himself;[1] otherwise he must of necessity be ruined. The principal foundations that all states have, new ones as well as old or mixed, are good laws and good arms. And because there cannot be good laws where there are not good arms, and where there are good arms there must be good laws, I shall leave out the reasoning on laws and shall speak of arms.

I say, therefore, that the arms with which a prince defends his state are either his own or mercenary or auxiliary or mixed. Mercenary and auxiliary arms are useless and dangerous; and if one keeps his state founded on mercenary arms, one will never be firm or secure; for they are disunited, ambitious, without discipline, unfaithful; bold among friends, among enemies cowardly; no fear of God, no faith with men; ruin is postponed only as long as attack is postponed; and in peace you are despoiled by them, in war by the enemy. The cause of this is that they have no love nor cause to keep them in the field other than a small stipend,

---

1. See Chapter 7.

which is not sufficient to make them want to die for you. They do indeed want to be your soldiers[2] while you are not making war, but when war comes, they either flee or leave. It should be little trouble for me to persuade anyone of this point, because the present ruin of Italy is caused by nothing other than its having relied for a period of many years on mercenary arms. These arms once made some progress for some, and may have appeared bold among themselves; but when the foreigner came, they showed what they were. Hence Charles, king of France, was allowed to seize Italy with chalk.[3] And he who said that our sins were the cause of it spoke the truth.[4] But the sins were surely not those he believed, but the ones I have told of, and because these were the sins of princes, they too have suffered the punishment for them.

I want to demonstrate better the failure of these arms. Mercenary captains are either excellent men of arms or not: if they are, you cannot trust them because they always aspire to their own greatness, either by oppressing you, who are their patron, or by oppressing others contrary to your intention; but if the captain is not virtuous, he ruins you in the ordinary way. And if one responds that whoever has arms in hand will do this, mercenary or not, I would reply that arms have to be employed either by a prince or by a republic. The prince should go in person, and perform himself the office of captain. The republic has to send its citizens, and when it sends one who does not turn out to be a

2. In the literal sense of "soldier": in your pay.

3. The chalk used to designate which houses would lodge French soldiers along their unresisted invasion route; the expression is attributed to Pope Alexander VI by the French historian Philippe de Commines in his *Memoirs*.

4. This was Savonarola in his sermon of November 1, 1494, who said that the French invasion was God's punishment of Italy and Florence. See *Discourses on Livy* I 11, 45, 56 for more of NM on Savonarola, and I 21; II 18 on the sins of Italian princes.

worthy man, it must change him; and if he is, it must check him with laws so that he does not step out of bounds. And by experience one sees that only princes and armed republics make very great progress; nothing but harm ever comes from mercenary arms. And a republic armed with its own arms is brought to obey one of its citizens with more difficulty than is a republic armed with foreign[5] arms.

Rome and Sparta stood for many centuries armed and free. The Swiss are very well armed and very free. The Carthaginians are an example of ancient mercenary arms; they were nearly oppressed by their own mercenary soldiers at the end of the first war with the Romans, even though the Carthaginians had their own citizens as heads.[6] After the death of Epaminondas, Philip of Macedon was made captain of their troops by the Thebans; and after his victory he took their liberty from them.[7] The Milanese, after Duke Filippo died, hired Francesco Sforza against the Venetians; when he had overcome the enemy at Caravaggio, he joined with them to oppress the Milanese, his patrons.[8] Sforza's father, in the hire of Queen Giovanna of Naples, at a stroke left her disarmed; then, so as not to lose the kingdom, she was compelled to throw herself in the lap of the king of Aragon.[9] And, if the Venetians and the Florentines have in the past increased their empire with these arms, and their captains did not thereupon make themselves princes but defended them, I respond that the Florentines

5. lit.: external
6. The Mercenary War at the end of the First Punic War, 241–237 B.C.
7. After Epaminondas's death in 362 B.C., Philip (who does not appear to have been a mercenary captain) became king of Macedon in 359 and occupied Thebes in 338.
8. The battle of Caravaggio took place in 1448; see NM's fuller account of Sforza's successful maneuver in *Florentine Histories* VI 18–22.
9. Muzio Attendolo Sforza (1369–1424); see *Florentine Histories* I 38.

were favored by chance in this case, because, of the virtuous captains whom they could have feared, some did not win, some had opposition, others turned their ambition elsewhere. The one who did not win was Giovanni Acuto.[10] Since he did not win, one could not know his faith, but everyone will confess that if he had won, the Florentines would have been at his discretion. Sforza always had the Bracceschi[11] against him, so that each watched the other: Francesco turned his ambition to Lombardy, Braccio against the Church and the kingdom of Naples.

But let us come to what happened a little while ago. The Florentines took as their captain Paolo Vitelli, a most prudent man who from private fortune had secured very great reputation. If he had captured Pisa, no one would deny that the Florentines would have had to stay with him, because if he had gone over in hire to their enemies, they would have had no remedy; and if they had kept him, they would have had to obey him. If one considers the progress of the Venetians, one will see that they acted securely and gloriously while they themselves made war (which was before they turned to enterprises on land). With their own gentry and armed plebs, they performed most virtuously, but when they began to fight on land, they left this virtue behind and they followed the customs of wars in Italy. And at the beginning of their expansion on land, because they did not have much of a state there and because they were held in great repute, they did not have much to fear from their captains; but as they expanded, which was under Carmagnola,[12] they suffered an instance of this error. For when they saw he was most virtuous, since the duke of Milan had

10. NM's rendering of the name of the English mercenary captain John Hawkwood.

11. Mercenaries of Andrea Fortebraccio, also known as Braccio da Montone; see *Florentine Histories* I 38, V 2.

12. Francesco di Bussone, count of Carmagnola (c1380–1432); see *Discourses on Livy* II 18.

been defeated by them under his government, and when they learned on the other hand that he had turned cool toward the war, they judged they could no longer win with him because he did not want to, nor could they dismiss him without losing what they had acquired. So in order to secure themselves, they were forced of necessity to kill him. Then they had as their captains Bartolomeo da Bergamo, Roberto da San Severino, the count of Pitigliano,[13] and such. With these they had to fear for loss, not for their gain, as then happened at Vailà: there they lost in one day what they had acquired with such trouble in eight hundred years. For these arms bring only slow, late, and weak acquisitions, but sudden and miraculous losses. And because with these examples I have come into Italy, which has been governed for many years by mercenary arms, I want to discourse on them more deeply, so that, when their origin and progress have been seen, one can correct them better.

So you[14] have to understand that in recent times as soon as Italy began to repel the empire, and the pope gained much reputation in temporal affairs, Italy divided into many states. For many of the large cities took up arms against their nobles, who formerly, supported by the emperor, had kept them under oppression; and the Church supported the cities to give herself reputation in temporal affairs. In many other cities their citizens became princes over them. Hence, since Italy had almost fallen into the hands of the Church and a few republics, and since the priests and the other citizens did not have knowledge of arms, they began to hire foreigners. The first who gave reputation to this kind of military was Alberigo da Conio,

13. Bartolomeo Colleoni, commander of the Venetian troops at Caravaggio (1448); Roberto da San Severino, commanding in the war against Ferrara (1482–84); Niccolò Orsini, count of Pitigliano, commanding at the battle of "Vailà" (Vailate) in 1509. See *Discourses on Livy* I 6, 53; III 31.
14. The formal or plural you.

from Romagna.[15] From his discipline came, among others, Braccio and Sforza, who in their times were the arbiters of Italy. After them came all the others who have governed these arms until our times. And the result of their virtue has been that Italy has been overrun by Charles, taken as booty by Louis, violated by Ferdinand, and insulted by the Swiss. The order they have held to has been, first, to take away reputation from the infantry in order to give reputation to themselves. They did this because they were men without a state who lived on industry. Having a few infantry did not give them reputation and they could not feed very many; so they were left with horse, and were fed and honored in tolerable number. And things came to the point that in an army of twenty thousand soldiers not two thousand infantry were to be found. Besides this, they had used all their industry to rid themselves and the soldiers of trouble and fear by not killing one another in battles but taking prisoners without asking ransom. They did not go against towns in the night; those in the towns would not go against their tents; around the camp they made neither stockade nor trench; they did not campaign in winter. And all these things were permitted in their military orders and discovered by them, as has been said, so as to escape trouble and dangers, so that they have led[16] Italy into slavery and disgrace.

15. Alberigo da Barbiano, count of Conio, died in 1409; on his Company of St. George, see NM, *Florentine Histories* I 34.
16. *condotta,* a pun on the contract (*condotta*) by which a *condottiere* is hired.

◆§ XIII ?◆

Of Auxiliary, Mixed, and One's Own Soldiers

Auxiliary arms, which are the other useless arms, are those of a power that is called to come with its arms to help and defend you, as was done by Pope Julius in recent times. When he had seen in the campaign of Ferrara the sad result of his mercenary arms, he turned to auxiliary ones; and he agreed with Ferdinand, king of Spain, that Ferdinand would help him with his men and armies. These arms can be useful and good in themselves, but for whoever calls them in, they are almost always harmful, because when they lose you are undone; when they win, you are left their prisoner. And although ancient histories are full of examples, nonetheless I do not wish to depart from this recent example of Pope Julius II, whose course of thrusting himself entirely into the hands of a foreigner, when he wanted Ferrara, could not have been less thought out. But his good fortune gave rise to a third thing so that he did not reap the fruit of his bad choice; for when his auxiliaries were defeated at Ravenna,[1] the Swiss rose up and, beyond all expectation, his own and others, drove out the victors; and he came out a prisoner neither of his enemies, who had fled, nor of his auxiliaries, since he had won with other arms than theirs. The Florentines, who were entirely unarmed, brought in ten thousand French to Pisa to capture it,[2] for which course they incurred more danger than in any other time of their travails. The emperor of Constantinople, so as to oppose his neighbors, sent ten thousand Turks into Greece; when the war was finished, they refused to leave.[3]

1. In 1512.
2. In 1500.
3. Emperor John Cantacuzene, in 1353.

This was the beginning of the servitude of Greece under the infidels.

Let him, then, who wants to be unable to win make use of these arms, since they are much more dangerous than mercenary arms. For with these, ruin is accomplished; they are all united, all resolved to obey someone else. But mercenary arms, when they have won, need more time and greater opportunity to hurt you, since they are not one whole body and have been found and paid for by you. In them the third party whom you may put at their head cannot quickly seize so much authority as to offend you. In sum, in mercenary arms laziness is more dangerous; in auxiliary arms, virtue is.

A wise prince, therefore, has always avoided these arms and turned to his own. He has preferred to lose with his own than to win with others, since he judges it no true victory that is acquired with alien arms. I shall never hesitate to cite Cesare Borgia and his actions. This duke came into Romagna with auxiliary arms, leading there entirely French troops, with whom he took Imola and Forlì. But when such arms no longer appeared safe to him, he turned to mercenaries, judging there to be less danger in them; and he hired the Orsini and Vitelli. Then in managing them, he found them doubtful, unfaithful, and dangerous; he eliminated them, and turned to his own arms. And one can easily see the difference between these arms if one considers what a difference there was in the reputation of the duke when he had only the French, and when he had the Orsini and Vitelli, and when he was left with his own soldiers and himself over them: his reputation will be found always to have increased, but he was never so much esteemed as when everyone saw that he was the total owner of his arms.

I did not want to depart from examples that are Italian and recent; yet I do not want to leave out Hiero of Syracuse, since he was one of those named above by me.[4] When he, as

4. In Chapter 6.

55

I said, was made head of the army by the Syracusans, he knew immediately that their mercenary military was not useful because they were condottieri set up like our Italians. Since he thought he could neither keep them nor let them go, he had them all cut to pieces, and then made war with his arms and not with alien arms. I want further to recall to memory a figure of the Old Testament apt for this purpose. When David offered to Saul to go and fight Goliath, the Philistine challenger, Saul, to give him spirit, armed him with his own arms—which David, as soon as he had them on, refused, saying that with them he could not give a good account of himself, and so he would rather meet the enemy with his sling and his knife.[5]

In fine, the arms of others either fall off your back or weigh you down or hold you tight. Charles VII, father of King Louis XI, who had liberated France from the English with his fortune and virtue, recognized this necessity of arming himself with his own arms, and laid down[6] an ordinance in his kingdom for men-at-arms and infantry. Then his son King Louis eliminated the ordinance for infantry and began to hire Swiss; this error, continued by others, is, as one sees now in fact, the cause of the dangers to that kingdom. For when he gave reputation to the Swiss, he debased all his own arms, because he had eliminated the infantry entirely and he had obligated his men-at-arms to the arms of others. For after they had become accustomed to fighting with Swiss, they did not think they could win without them. From this it follows that French are not enough against Swiss and without Swiss do not try against anyone else. Thus, the armies of France have been mixed, part mercenary and part their own. These arms all together are much better than simple auxiliary or simple mercenary

5. NM's account of this episode differs significantly from the biblical original in 1 Samuel 17: 38–40, 50–51.
6. lit.: ordered.

arms, but much inferior to one's own. And the example given is enough, because the kingdom of France would be unconquerable if the ordering of Charles had been expanded or preserved. But lack of prudence in men begins something in which, because it tastes good then, they do not perceive the poison that lies underneath, as I said above of consumptive fevers.[7]

Therefore, he who does not recognize evils when they arise in a principality is not truly wise, and this is given to few. And if one considers the first cause of the ruin of the Roman Empire, one will find it to have begun only with the hiring of Goths, because from that beginning the forces of the Roman Empire began to weaken, and all the virtue that was taken from it was given to them.

I conclude, thus, that without its own arms no principality is secure; indeed it is wholly obliged to fortune since it does not have virtue to defend itself[8] in adversity. And it has always been the opinion and judgment of wise men "that nothing is so infirm and unstable as fame for power not sustained by one's own force."[9] And one's own arms are those which are composed of either subjects or citizens or your creatures: all others are either mercenary or auxiliary. And the mode of ordering one's own arms will be easy to find if one reviews[10] the orders of the four I have named above[11] and if one sees how Philip, father of Alexander the Great, and how many republics and princes have armed and ordered themselves. I submit myself entirely to these orders.

7. In Chapter 3, where NM referred to diseases, not to remedies.

8. One manuscript has "with faith" at this point.

9. Quoted by NM in Latin from Tacitus, *Annals* XIII.19; the words *rerum mortalium* ("of mortal things") have been omitted by NM after "nothing."

10. lit.: discourses on.

11. The four named in this chapter are Cesare Borgia, Hiero, David, and Charles VII. In Chapter 6 NM mentions Moses, Cyrus, Romulus, and Theseus.

❧ XIV ❧

What a Prince Should Do
Regarding the Military

Thus, a prince should have no other object, nor any other thought, nor take anything else as his art but that of war and its orders and discipline; for that is the only art which is of concern to one who commands. And it is of such virtue that not only does it maintain those who have been born princes but many times it enables men of private fortune to rise to that rank; and on the contrary, one sees that when princes have thought more of amenities than of arms, they have lost their states. And the first cause that makes you lose it is the neglect of this art; and the cause that enables you to acquire it is to be a professional in this art.

Francesco Sforza, because he was armed, became duke of Milan from a private individual; and his sons, because they shunned the hardships of arms, became private individuals from dukes.[1] For, among the other causes of evil that being unarmed brings you, it makes you contemptible, which is one of those infamies the prince should be on guard against, as will be said below. For there is no proportion between one who is armed and one who is unarmed, and it is not reasonable that whoever is armed obey willingly whoever is unarmed, and that someone unarmed be secure among armed servants. For since there is scorn in the one and suspicion in the other, it is not possible for them to work well together. And therefore a prince who does not understand the military, besides other unhappiness, cannot, as was said, be esteemed by his soldiers nor have trust in them.

1. Francesco Sforza's "sons" (rather, his descendants) were Galeazzo Maria, murdered in 1476; Gian Galeazzo, deposed by his uncle Ludovico il Moro in 1480; and Ludovico il Moro, deposed in 1500. The emperor Maximilian I, deposed in 1515, may perhaps be included.

Therefore, he should never lift his thoughts from the exercise of war, and in peace he should exercise it more than in war. This he can do in two modes, one with deeds, the other with the mind. And as to deeds, besides keeping his armies well ordered and exercised, he should always be out hunting, and through this accustom the body to hardships; and meanwhile he should learn the nature of sites, and recognize how mountains rise, how valleys open up, how plains lie, and understand the nature of rivers and marshes—and in this invest the greatest care. This knowledge is useful in two modes. First, one learns to know one's own country, and one can better understand its defense; then, through the knowledge of and experience with those sites, one can comprehend with ease every other site that it may be necessary to explore[2] as new. For the hills, the valleys, the plains, the rivers, and the marshes that are in Tuscany, for example, have a certain similarity to those of other provinces, so that from the knowledge of a site in one province one can easily come to the knowledge of others. And the prince who lacks this skill lacks the first part of what a captain must have, for this teaches him to find the enemy, seize lodgings, lead armies, order battles, and besiege towns to your advantage.[3]

Among other praise given by writers to Philopoemen, prince of the Achaeans,[4] is that in times of peace he never thought of anything but modes of war; and when he was on campaign with friends, he often stopped and reasoned with them: "If the enemy were on top of that hill and we were here with our army, which of us would have the advantage? How could one advance to meet them while maintaining

2. lit.: speculate on.
3. On knowledge of the nature of sites as "science," see *Discourses on Livy* III 39; and see the Dedicatory Letter above.
4. Philopoemen (253–183 B.C.), a head of the Achaean League. The writers who praise him are Livy (XXXV.28) and Plutarch (*Life of Philopoemen*, 4).

order? If we wanted to retreat from here, how would we have to do it? If they retreated, how would we have to follow them?" And he put before them, as he went along, all the chances that can occur to an army; he listened to their opinions, gave his own, supported it with reasons, so that because of these continued cogitations there could never arise, while he led the army, any accident for which he did not have the remedy.

But, as to the exercise of the mind, a prince should read histories and consider in them the actions of excellent men, should see how they conducted themselves in wars, should examine the causes of their victories and losses, so as to be able to avoid the latter and imitate the former. Above all he should do as some excellent man has done in the past who found someone to imitate who had been praised and glorified before him, whose exploits and actions he always kept beside himself, as they say Alexander the Great imitated Achilles; Caesar, Alexander; Scipio, Cyrus. And whoever reads the life of Cyrus written by Xenophon[5] will then recognize in the life of Scipio how much glory that imitation brought him, how much in chastity, affability, humanity, and liberality Scipio conformed to what had been written of Cyrus by Xenophon.

A wise prince should observe such modes, and never remain idle in peaceful times, but with his industry make capital of them in order to be able to profit from them in adversities, so that when fortune changes, it will find him ready to resist them.

5. The title of Xenophon's book is actually *Cyropaideia,* "The Education of Cyrus."

Of Those Things for Which Men And Especially Princes Are Praised or Blamed

It remains now to see what the modes and government of a prince should be with subjects and with friends. And because I know that many have written of this, I fear that in writing of it again, I may be held presumptuous, especially since in disputing this matter I depart from the orders of others. But since my intent is to write something useful to whoever understands it, it has appeared to me more fitting to go directly to the effectual truth of the thing than to the imagination of it. And many have imagined republics and principalities that have never been seen or known to exist in truth; for it is so far from how one lives to how one should live that he who lets go of what is done for what should be done learns his ruin rather than his preservation. For a man who wants to make a profession of good in all regards must come to ruin among so many who are not good. Hence it is necessary to a prince, if he wants to maintain himself, to learn to be able not to be good, and to use this and not use it according to necessity.

Thus, leaving out what is imagined about a prince and discussing what is true, I say that all men, whenever one speaks of them, and especially princes, since they are placed higher, are noted for some of the qualities that bring them either blame or praise. And this is why someone is considered liberal, someone mean (using a Tuscan term because *avaro* [avaricious] in our language is still one who desires to have something by rapine, *misero* [mean] we call one who refrains too much from using what is his); someone is considered a giver, someone rapacious; someone cruel, someone merciful;[1] the one a breaker of faith, the other faithful; the one effeminate and pusillanimous, the other fierce and spirited; the one humane, the other proud; the one lascivious, the other chaste; the one honest, the other astute; the one hard, the other agreeable;[2] the one grave, the other light; the one religious, the other unbelieving, and the like. And I know that everyone will confess that it would be a very praiseworthy thing to find in a prince all of the above-mentioned qualities that are held good. But because he cannot have them, nor wholly[3] observe them, since human conditions do not permit it, it is necessary for him to be so prudent as to know how to avoid the infamy of those vices that would take his state from him and to be on guard against those that do not, if that is possible; but if one cannot, one can let them go on with less hesitation. And furthermore one should not care about incurring the fame[4] of those vices without which it is difficult to save one's state; for if one considers everything well, one will find something appears to be virtue, which if pursued would be one's ruin, and something else appears to be vice, which if pursued results in one's security and well-being.

1. *pietoso* has a connotation of "pious."
2. lit.: easy.
3. Or honestly.
4. Some manuscripts have *infamia,* "infamy."

❧§ XVI ॐ

[reluctance to spend]

Of Liberality and Parsimony

Beginning, then, with the first of the above-mentioned qualities, I say that it would be good to be held liberal; nonetheless, liberality, when used so that you may be held liberal, hurts[1] you. For if it is used virtuously and as it should be used, it may not be recognized, and you will not escape the infamy of its contrary. And so, if one wants to maintain a name for liberality among men, it is necessary not to leave out any kind of lavish display, so that a prince who has done this will always consume all his resources in such deeds. In the end it will be necessary, if he wants to maintain a name for liberality, to burden the people extraordinarily, to be rigorous with taxes, and to do all those things that can be done to get money. This will begin to make him hated by his subjects, and little esteemed by anyone as he becomes poor; so having offended the many and rewarded the few with this liberality of his, he feels every least hardship and runs into risk at every slight danger. When he recognizes this, and wants to draw back from it, he immediately incurs the infamy of meanness.

Thus, since a prince cannot, without damage to himself, use the virtue of liberality so that it is recognized, he should not, if he is prudent, care about a name for meanness. For with time he will always be held more and more liberal when it is seen that with his parsimony his income is enough for him, that he can defend himself from whoever makes war on him, and that he can undertake campaigns without burdening the people. So he comes to use liberality with all those from whom he does not take, who are infinite, and meanness with all those to whom he does not give, who are few. In our times we have not seen great things done except by those who have been considered mean; the others have been eliminated. Pope Julius II, while he made use of a name for liberality to attain the papacy, did not think of maintaining it later, so as to be able to make war. The present king of France[2] has carried on many wars without imposing an extraordinary tax on his subjects, only because

1. lit.: offends.
2. Louis XII.

the extra expenses were administered with his long-practiced parsimony. If the present king of Spain[3] had been held liberal, he would not have been able to make or win so many campaigns.

Therefore, so as not to have to rob his subjects, to be able to defend himself, not to become poor and contemptible, nor to be forced to become rapacious, a prince should esteem it little to incur a name for meanness, because this is one of those vices which enable him to rule. And if someone should say: Caesar attained empire with liberality, and many others, because they have been and have been held to be liberal, have attained very great rank, I respond: either you are already a prince or you are on the path to acquiring it: in the first case this liberality is damaging; in the second it is indeed necessary to be held liberal. And Caesar was one of those who wanted to attain the principate of Rome; but if after he had arrived there, had he remained alive and not been temperate with his expenses, he would have destroyed that empire. And if someone should reply: many have been princes and have done great things with their armies who have been held very liberal, I respond to you: either the prince spends from what is his own and his subjects' or from what belongs to someone else. In the first case he should be sparing; in the other, he should not leave out any part of liberality. And for the prince who goes out with his armies, who feeds on booty, pillage, and ransom and manages on what belongs to someone else, this liberality is necessary; otherwise he would not be followed by his soldiers. And of what is not yours or your subjects' one can be a bigger giver, as were Cyrus, Caesar, and Alexander, because spending what is someone else's does not take reputation from you but adds it to you; only spending your own is what harms you. And there is nothing that consumes itself as much as liberality: while you use it, you lose the capacity to

3. Ferdinand the Catholic.

use it; and you become either poor and contemptible or, to escape poverty, rapacious and hateful. Among all the things that a prince should guard against is being contemptible and hated, and liberality leads you to both. So there is more wisdom in maintaining a name for meanness, which begets infamy without hatred, than in being under a necessity, because one wants to have a name for liberality, to incur a name for rapacity, which begets infamy with hatred.

⚜ XVII ⚜

Of Cruelty and Mercy,[1] and Whether It Is Better to Be Loved Than Feared, or the Contrary

Descending next to the other qualities cited before, I say that each prince should desire to be held merciful and not cruel; nonetheless he should take care not to use this mercy badly. Cesare Borgia was held to be cruel; nonetheless his cruelty restored the Romagna, united it, and reduced it to peace and to faith. If one considers this well, one will see that he was much more merciful than the Florentine people, who so as to escape a name for cruelty, allowed Pistoia to be destroyed.[2] A prince, therefore, so as to keep his subjects united and faithful, should not care about the infamy of cruelty, because with very few examples he will be more merciful than those who for the sake of too much mercy allow disorders to continue, from which come killings or

1. Or piety, throughout *The Prince*.
2. From 1500 to 1502 Pistoia, a city subject to Florence, was torn by factional disputes and riots. NM was there as representative of the Florentines on several occasions in 1501.

robberies; for these customarily hurt[3] a whole community,[4] but the executions that come from the prince hurt[5] one particular person. And of all princes, it is impossible for the new prince to escape a name for cruelty because new states are full of dangers. And Virgil says in the mouth of Dido: "The harshness of things and the newness of the kingdom compel me to contrive such things, and to keep a broad watch over the borders."[6]

Nonetheless, he should be slow to believe and to move, nor should he make himself feared, and he should proceed in a temperate mode with prudence and humanity so that too much confidence does not make him incautious and too much diffidence does not render him intolerable.

From this a dispute arises whether it is better to be loved than feared, or the reverse. The response is that one would want to be both the one and the other; but because it is difficult to put them together, it is much safer to be feared than loved, if one has to lack one of the two. For one can say this generally of men: that they are ungrateful, fickle, pretenders and dissemblers, evaders of danger, eager for gain. While you do them good, they are yours, offering you their blood, property, lives, and children, as I said above,[7] when the need for them is far away; but, when it is close to you, they revolt. And that prince who has founded himself entirely on their words, stripped of other preparation, is ruined; for friendships that are acquired at a price and not with greatness and nobility of spirit are bought, but they are not owned and when the time comes they cannot be spent. And men have less hesitation to offend one who makes himself loved than one who makes himself feared; for love is held by a chain of obligation, which, because men are

3. lit.: offend.
4. lit.: a whole universality.
5. lit.: offend.
6. Virgil, *Aeneid* I 563–64.
7. See Chapter 9.

wicked, is broken at every opportunity for their own utility, but fear is held by a dread of punishment that never forsakes you.

The prince should nonetheless make himself feared in such a mode that if he does not acquire love, he escapes hatred, because being feared and not being hated can go together very well. This he will always do if he abstains from the property of his citizens and his subjects, and from their women; and if he also needs to proceed against someone's life,[8] he must do it when there is suitable justification and manifest cause for it. But above all, he must abstain from the property of others, because men forget the death of a father more quickly than the loss of a patrimony. Furthermore, causes for taking away property are never lacking, and he who begins to live by rapine always finds cause to seize others' property; and, on the contrary, causes for taking life[9] are rarer and disappear more quickly.

But when the prince is with his armies and has a multitude of soldiers under his government, then it is above all necessary not to care about a name for cruelty, because without this name he never holds his army united, or disposed to any action. Among the admirable actions of Hannibal is numbered this one: that when he had a very large army, mixed with infinite kinds of men, and had led it to fight in alien lands, no dissension ever arose in it, neither among themselves nor against the prince, in bad as well as in his good fortune. This could not have arisen from anything other than his inhuman cruelty which, together with his infinite virtues, always made him venerable and terrible in the sight of his soldiers; and without it, his other virtues would not have sufficed to bring about this effect. And the writers, having considered little in this, on the one hand admire this action of his but on the other condemn the principal cause of it.

8. lit.: blood.
9. lit.: blood.

67

And to see that it is true that his other virtues would not have been enough, one can consider Scipio, who was very rare not only in his times but also in the entire memory of things known—whose armies in Spain rebelled against him. This arose from nothing but his excessive mercy, which had allowed his soldiers more license than is fitting for military discipline. Scipio's mercy was reproved in the Senate by Fabius Maximus, who called him the corruptor of the Roman military. After the Locrians had been destroyed by a legate of Scipio's, they were not avenged by him, nor was the insolence of that legate corrected—all of which arose from his agreeable nature, so that when someone in the Senate wanted to excuse him, he said that there were many men who knew better how not to err than how to correct errors. Such a nature would in time have sullied Scipio's fame and glory if he had continued with it in the empire; but while he lived under the government of the Senate, this damaging quality of his not only was hidden, but made for his glory.[10]

I conclude, then, returning to being feared and loved, that since men love at their convenience and fear at the convenience of the prince, a wise prince should found himself on what is his, not on what is someone else's; he should only contrive to avoid hatred, as was said.

10. On the comparison between Hannibal and Scipio, see also *Discourses on Livy* III 19–21. NM's source is in Livy, XXIX 19, 21.

৺ XVIII ঽ৵

In What Mode Faith Should Be Kept by Princes

How praiseworthy it is for a prince to keep his faith, and to live with honesty and not by astuteness, everyone understands. Nonetheless one sees by experience in our times that the princes who have done great things are those who have taken little account of faith and have known how to get around men's brains with their astuteness; and in the end they have overcome those who have founded themselves on loyalty.

Thus, you[1] must know that there are two kinds of combat: one with laws, the other with force. The first is proper to man, the second to beasts; but because the first is often not enough, one must have recourse to the second. Therefore it is necessary for a prince to know well how to use the beast and the man. This role was taught covertly to princes by ancient writers, who wrote that Achilles, and many other ancient princes, were given to Chiron the centaur to be raised, so that he would look after them with his discipline. To have as teacher a half-beast, half-man means nothing other than that a prince needs to know how to use both natures; and the one without the other is not lasting.

Thus, since a prince is compelled of necessity to know well how to use the beast, he should pick the fox and the lion,[2] because the lion does not defend itself from snares and the fox does not defend itself from wolves. So one needs to be a fox to recognize snares and a lion to frighten the wolves. Those who stay simply with the lion do not understand this. A prudent lord, therefore, cannot observe faith, nor should he, when such observance turns against him, and the causes that made him promise have been eliminated. And if all men were good, this teaching would not be good; but because they are wicked and do not observe faith with you, you also do not have to observe it with them. Nor does a prince ever lack legitimate causes to color his failure to observe faith. One could give infinite modern examples of this, and show how many peace treaties and promises have been rendered invalid and

---

1. The formal or plural you.
2. A possible source for this: Cicero, De Officiis I.11.34; 13.41.

vain through the infidelity of princes; and the one who has known best how to use the fox has come out best. But it is necessary to know well how to color this nature, and to be a great pretender and dissembler; and men are so simple and so obedient to present necessities that he who deceives will always find someone who will let himself be deceived.

I do not want to be silent about one of the recent examples. Alexander VI never did anything, nor ever thought of anything, but how to deceive men, and he always found a subject to whom he could do it. And there never was a man with greater efficacy in asserting a thing, and in affirming it with greater oaths, who observed it less; nonetheless, his deceits succeeded at his will, because he well knew this aspect of the world.

Thus, it is not necessary for a prince to have all the above-mentioned qualities in fact, but it is indeed necessary to appear to have them. Nay, I dare say this, that by having them and always observing them, they are harmful; and by appearing to have them, they are useful, as it is to appear merciful, faithful, humane, honest, and religious, and to be so; but to remain with a spirit built so that, if you need not to be those things, you are able and know how to change to the contrary. This has to be understood: that a prince, and especially a new prince, cannot observe all those things for which men are held good, since he is often under a necessity, to maintain his state, of acting against faith, against charity, against humanity, against religion. And so he needs to have a spirit disposed to change as the winds of fortune and variations of things command him, and as I said above, not depart from good, when possible, but know how to enter into evil, when forced by necessity.

A prince should thus take great care that nothing escape his mouth that is not full of the above-mentioned five qualities and that, to see him and hear him, he should appear all mercy, all faith, all honesty, all humanity, all religion. And nothing is more necessary to appear to have than this last quality. Men in general[3] judge more by their eyes than by their hands, because seeing is given[4] to everyone, touching to few. Everyone sees how you appear, few touch what you are; and these few dare not oppose the opinion of many, who have the majesty of the state to defend them; and in the actions of all men, and especially of princes, where there is no court to appeal to, one looks to the end. So let a prince win and maintain his state: the means will always be judged honorable, and will be praised by everyone. For the vulgar are taken in by the appearance and the outcome of a thing, and in the world there is no one but the vulgar; the few have a place there[5] when the many have somewhere to lean on. A certain prince of present times, whom it is not well to name,[6] never preaches anything but peace and faith, and is very hostile to both. If he had observed both, he would have had either his reputation or his state taken from him many times.

3. lit.: universally.
4. lit.: touches.
5. One manuscript says "the few have no place there . . ."; and the authorities have divided, Casella, Russo, and Sasso accepting "no place," Chabod and Bertelli "a place."
6. Apparently Ferdinand the Catholic, whom NM unhesitatingly names in Chapter 21.

❧ XIX ☙

Of Avoiding Contempt and Hatred

But because I have spoken of the most important of the qualities mentioned above, I want to discourse on the others briefly under this generality, that the prince, as was said above in part, should think how to avoid those things that make him hateful and contemptible. When he avoids them, he will have done his part and will find no danger in his other infamies. What makes him hated above all, as I said,[1] is to be rapacious and a usurper of the property and the women of his subjects. From these he must abstain, and whenever one does not take away either property or honor from the generality[2] of men, they live content and one has only to combat the ambition of the few which may be checked in many modes and with ease. What makes him contemptible is to be held variable, light, effeminate, pusillanimous, irresolute, from which a prince should guard himself as from a shoal. He should contrive that greatness, spiritedness, gravity, and strength are recognized in his actions, and he should insist that his judgments in the private concerns of his subjects be irrevocable. And he should maintain such an opinion of himself that no one thinks either of deceiving him or of getting around him.

The prince who gives this opinion of himself is highly reputed, and against whoever is reputed it is difficult to conspire, difficult to mount an attack, provided it is understood that he is excellent and revered by his own subjects. For a prince should have two fears: one within, on account of his subjects; the other outside, on account of external powers. From the latter one is defended with good arms and good friends; and if one has good arms, one will always have good friends. And things inside will always remain steady, if things outside are steady, unless indeed they are disturbed by a conspiracy; and even if things outside are in motion, provided he has ordered and lived as I said, as long as he does not forsake himself he will always withstand every thrust, as I said Nabis the Spartan did.[3] But, as to

1. See Chapter 17 above.
2. lit. universality.
3. Chapter 9 above, where Nabis is featured as a prince of a civil principality. NM does not disclose here, as he does in *Discourses on Livy* III 6, that Nabis was in fact killed by a conspiracy.

subjects, when things outside are not moving, one has to fear that they may be conspiring secretly. From this the prince may secure himself sufficiently if he avoids being hated or despised and keeps the people satisfied with him; this is necessary to achieve, as was said above at length.[4] And one of the most powerful remedies that a prince has against conspiracies is not to be hated by the people generally.[5] For whoever conspires always believes he will satisfy the people with the death of the prince, but when he believes he will offend them, he does not get up the spirit to adopt such a course, because the difficulties on the side of the conspirators are infinite. And one sees from experience that there have been many conspiracies, but few have had a good end. For whoever conspires cannot be alone, but he cannot find company except from those he believes to be malcontents; and as soon as you disclose your intent to a malcontent, you give him the matter with which to become content, because manifestly he can hope for every advantage from it. So, seeing sure gain on this side, and on the other, dubious gain full of danger, he must indeed either be a rare friend, or an altogether obstinate enemy of the prince, to observe his faith with you. And to reduce this to brief terms, I say that on the part of the conspirator there is nothing but fear, jealousy, and the anticipation of terrifying punishment; but on the part of the prince there is the majesty of the principality, the laws, the protection of friends and of the state which defend him, so that when popular good will is added to all these things, it is impossible that anyone should be so rash as to conspire. For whereas a conspirator ordinarily has to fear before the execution of the evil, in this case (having the people as enemies) he must fear afterwards too, when the excess has occurred, nor can he hope for any refuge.

4. Chapters 16, 17.
5. lit.: by the universal.

One might give infinite examples of this matter, but I wish to be content with only one that happened within the memory of our fathers. Messer Annibale Bentivoglio, grandfather of the present Messer Annibale, who was prince in Bologna, was killed by the Canneschi conspiring against him, and no one survived him but Messer Giovanni, who was in swaddling clothes. Immediately after that homicide the people rose up and killed all the Canneschi. This came from the popular good will the house of Bentivoglio had in those times, which was so great that since there remained no one of that house in Bologna who could rule the state, Annibale being dead, and since there was indication that in Florence someone had been born of the Bentivogli who was considered until then the son of a blacksmith, the Bolognese came to Florence for him and gave him the government of their city, which was governed by him until Messer Giovanni reached an age suitable for governing.[6]

I conclude, therefore, that a prince should take little account of conspiracies if the people show good will to him; but if they are hostile and bear hatred for him, he should fear everything and everyone. And well-ordered states and wise princes have thought out with all diligence how not to make the great desperate and how to satisfy the people and keep them content, because this is one of the most important matters that concern a prince.

Among the well-ordered and governed kingdoms in our times is that of France;[7] and in it are infinite good institutions on which the liberty and security of the king depend. The first of these is the parlement and its authority. For the one who ordered that kingdom,[8] knowing the am-

6. See NM, *Florentine Histories* VI 9–10.

7. On the kingdom of France, see also *Discourses on Livy* I 16, 17, 55; and NM's *Ritratto di cose di Francia*.

8. Perhaps a reference to Louis IX, by whom the Parlement of Paris was organized out of the preceding king's court. Parlements in the French monarchy were law courts, not legislative assemblies.

bition of the powerful and their insolence, and judging it necessary for them to have a bit in their mouths to correct them, and on the other side, knowing the hatred of the generality of people[9] against the great, which is founded in its fear, and wanting to secure them, intended this not to be the particular concern of the king, so as to take from him the blame he would have from the great when he favored the popular side, and from the popular side when he favored the great; and so he constituted a third judge to be the one who would beat down the great and favor the lesser side without blame for the king. This order could not be better, or more prudent, or a greater cause of the security of the king and the kingdom. From this one can infer another notable thing: that princes should have anything blameable administered by others, favors[10] by themselves. Again I conclude that a prince should esteem the great, but not make himself hated by the people.

It might perhaps appear to many, considering the life and death of some Roman emperor, that there were examples contrary to my opinion, since one may find someone who has always lived excellently, and shown great virtue of spirit, and has nonetheless lost the empire or indeed been killed by his own subjects who conspired against him. Since I want, therefore, to respond to these objections, I shall discuss the qualities of certain emperors, showing the causes of their ruin to be not unlike that which I have advanced; and in part I shall offer for consideration things that are notable for whoever reads about the actions of those times. And I want it to suffice for me to take all the emperors who succeeded to the empire, from Marcus the philosopher to Maximinus: these were Marcus, Commodus his son, Pertinax, Julianus, Severus, his son Antoninus Caracalla, Macrinus, Heliogabalus, Alexander,[11] and Max-

9. lit.: of the universal.
10. lit.: things of grace.
11. Alexander Severus.

iminus. And first it is to be noted that whereas in other principalities one has to contend only with the ambition of the great and the insolence of the people, the Roman emperors had a third difficulty, of having to bear with the cruelty and avarice of their soldiers. This was so difficult that it was the cause of the ruin of many, since it was difficult to satisfy the soldiers and the people. For the people loved quiet, and therefore loved modest princes, and the soldiers loved a prince with a military spirit who was insolent, cruel, and rapacious. They wanted him to practice these things on the people so that they could double their pay and give vent to their avarice and cruelty. These things always brought about the ruin of those emperors who by nature or by art did not have a great reputation such that they could hold both in check. And most of them, especially those who came to the principate as new men, once they recognized the difficulty of these two diverse humors, turned to satisfying the soldiers, caring little about injuring the people. This course was necessary; for since princes cannot fail to be hated by someone, they are at first forced not to be hated by the people generally;[12] and when they cannot continue this, they have to contrive with all industry to avoid the hatred of those communities which are most powerful. And so those emperors who because they were new had need of extraordinary support stuck to the soldiers rather than the people, which nonetheless turned out useful for them or not according to whether that prince knew how to keep himself in repute with them. From the causes mentioned above, Marcus, Pertinax, and Alexander, all living a modest life, lovers of justice, enemies of cruelty, humane

12. *università* is singular here, according to some MSS accepted by Chabod; it is plural and translated as "communities" in the next clause; *università* is derived from the medieval Latin *universitas,* which means both a legal body or corporation and (sometimes) the community on which such bodies depend. NM's usage lacks the legalism of medieval usage.

and kind, all, except for Marcus, came to a bad end. Only Marcus lived and died most honorably, because he succeeded to the empire by hereditary right and did not have to acknowledge it as from either the soldiers or the people; then, since he was attended with many virtues that made him venerable, while he lived he always kept the one order and the other within its bounds, and was never either hated or despised. But Pertinax was created emperor against the will of the soldiers, who, since they were used to living in license under Commodus, could not tolerate the decent life to which Pertinax wanted to return them; hence, having created hatred for himself, and to this hatred added disdain since he was old, he was ruined in the first beginnings of his administration.

And here one should note that hatred is acquired through good deeds as well as bad ones; and so, as I said above,[13] a prince who wants to maintain his state is often forced not to be good. For when that community[14] of which you judge you have need to maintain yourself is corrupt, whether they are the people or the soldiers or the great, you must follow their humor to satisfy them, and then good deeds are your enemy. But let us come to Alexander. He was of such goodness that among the other praise attributed to him is this: that in the fourteen years he held the empire no one was ever put to death by him without a trial. Nonetheless, since he was held to be effeminate and a man who let himself be governed by his mother, and for this came to be despised, the army conspired against him and killed him.

Reviewing[15] now, by contrast, the qualities of Commodus, of Severus,[16] Antoninus Caracalla, and Max-

13. Chapter 15.
14. See note 12 above.
15. lit.: discoursing on.
16. Septimius Severus, who in *Discourses on Livy* I 10 is called a criminal.

iminus, you[17] will find them very cruel and very rapacious. To satisfy the soldiers, they would not spare any kind of injury that could be inflicted on the people; and all except Severus came to a bad end. For in Severus was so much virtue that, by keeping the soldiers his friends, although the people were overburdened by him, he was always able to rule happily because his virtues made him so admirable in the sight of the soldiers and the people that the latter remained somehow astonished and stupefied, while the former were reverent and satisfied.

And because the actions of this man were great and notable in a new prince, I want to show briefly how well he knew how to use the persons of the fox and the lion, whose natures I say above[18] are necessary for a prince to imitate. Since Severus knew of the indolence of Emperor Julianus, he persuaded his army, of which he was captain in Slavonia, that it would be good to go to Rome and avenge the death of Pertinax, who had been put to death by the praetorian soldiers. Under this pretext, without showing that he aspired to the empire, he moved his army against Rome; and he was in Italy before his departure was known. When he arrived at Rome, he was elected emperor by the Senate out of fear and Julianus put to death. After this beginning there remained two difficulties for Severus if he wanted to become lord of the whole state: one in Asia, where Pescennius Niger, the head of the Asian armies, had had himself called emperor; and the other in the West, where Albinus also aspired to the empire. And because he judged it dangerous to disclose himself as an enemy to both, he decided to attack Niger and deceive Albinus. To Albinus he wrote that since he had been elected emperor by the Senate he wanted to share that dignity with him; he sent him the title of Caesar, and by decision of the Senate accepted him as colleague. These

17. The formal or plural you.
18. Chapter 18.

things were accepted by Albinus as true. But after Severus had defeated Niger, put him to death, and brought peace to affairs in the East, he returned to Rome and complained in the Senate that Albinus, hardly grateful for the benefits he had received from him, had perfidiously sought to kill him, and for this it was necessary for Severus to go punish his ingratitude. Then he went to meet him in France, and took from him his state and his life.

Thus, whoever examines minutely the actions of this man will find him a very fierce lion and a very astute fox, will see that he was feared and revered by everyone, and not hated by the army, and will not marvel that he, a new man, could have held so much power.[19] For his very great reputation always defended him from the hatred that the people could have conceived for him because of his robberies. But his son Antoninus [Caracalla] was himself a man who had most excellent parts that made him marvelous in the sight of the people and pleasing to the soldiers. For he was a military man, very capable of enduring every trouble, disdainful of all delicate food and of all other softness, which made him loved by all the armies. Nonetheless, his ferocity and cruelty were so great and so unheard of—for after infinite individual killings he had put to death a great part of the people of Rome and all the people of Alexandria—that he became most hateful to all the world. He began to be feared even by those whom he had around him, so that he was killed by a centurion in the midst of his army. Here it is to be noted that deaths such as these, which follow from the decision of an obstinate spirit, cannot be avoided by princes because anyone who does not care about death can hurt[20] him; but the prince may well fear them less because they are very rare. He should only guard against doing grave injury to anyone of those whom he uses and has around him in the

19. lit.: empire.
20. lit.: offend.

service of his principality, as Antoninus had done. He had put to death with disgrace a brother of that centurion, and threatened him every day; yet he kept him in his bodyguard, which was a rash policy likely to bring ruin, as happened to him.[21]

But let us come to Commodus, who held the empire with great ease because he had it by hereditary right, being the son of Marcus. It was enough for him only to follow in the footsteps of his father, and he would have satisfied both the soldiers and the people. But since he had a cruel and bestial spirit, so as to practice his rapacity on the people he turned to indulging the armies and making them licentious. On the other hand, by not keeping his dignity, by descending often into theaters to fight with gladiators, and by doing other very base things hardly deserving of the imperial majesty, he became contemptible in the sight of the soldiers. And since he was hated on one side and despised on the other, he was conspired against and put to death.

It remains now to tell of the qualities of Maximinus. He was a very warlike man; and since the armies were disgusted with the softness of Alexander, whom I discussed above, when he was put to death they elected Maximinus to the empire. He did not possess it for long because two things made him hated and contemptible: one was being of very base origin[22] because he had formerly herded sheep in Thrace (which was very well known everywhere and brought great disdain for him in the sight of everyone); the other was that because at the start of his principality he had deferred going to Rome and taking possession of the imperial throne, he had established an opinion of himself as very

21. See also *Discourses on Livy* III 6, where NM says that the centurion was the instrument or executive of another conspirator, Macrinus, who was Caracalla's prefect and is not said to have suffered "grave injury" from Caracalla. Macrinus proclaimed himself emperor in 217 and was overthrown in 218.

22. lit.: being very base.

cruel, since he had committed many cruelties through his prefects in Rome and everywhere in the empire. So, since the whole world was excited by indignation at the baseness of his blood and by hatred arising from fear of his ferocity, Africa rebelled first, then the Senate with all the people of Rome; and all Italy conspired against him. These were joined by his own army, which, while besieging Aquileia and finding difficulty in capturing it, became disgusted with this cruelty, and fearing him less because it saw he had so many enemies, it killed him.

I do not want to reason about either Heliogabalus or Macrinus or Julianus, who, because they were altogether contemptible, were immediately eliminated; but I shall come to the conclusion of this discourse. And I say that the princes of our times have less of this difficulty of satisfying the soldiers by extraordinary means in their governments. For notwithstanding that one has to show them some consideration, yet this is quickly settled because none of these princes has armies joined together which are entrenched in the government and administration of provinces, as were the armies of the Roman Empire. And so, if at that time it was necessary to satisfy the soldiers rather than the people, it was because the soldiers could do more than the people. Now it is necessary for all princes except the Turk and the Sultan[23] to satisfy the people rather than the soldiers, because the people can do more than the soldiers. I except the Turk from this, since he always keeps around him twelve thousand infantry and fifteen thousand horse on whom the security and strength of his kingdom depend; and it is necessary for that lord to put off every other regard and

---

23. Apparently "the Turk" is Selim I, sultan of the Ottoman Turks from 1512 to 1520, and "the Sultan" is the last sultan of the Mamelukes in Egypt, Tuman Bey, who was overthrown by Selim I in 1517. Selim I is called "the Grand Turk" by NM in the *Discourses on Livy*: see I 1, 19, 30; II 17; III 6, 35.

keep them his friends. Similarly, since the kingdom of the sultan is in the hands of the soldiers, he also is required to keep them his friends, without respect for the people. And you[24] have to note that the sultan's state is formed unlike all other principalities because it is similar to the Christian pontificate, which cannot be called either a hereditary principality or a new principality. For it is not the sons of the old prince who are the heirs and become the lords, but the one who is elected to that rank by those who have the authority for it. And this being an ancient order, one cannot call it a new principality, because some of the difficulties in new principalities are not in it; for if the prince is indeed new, the orders of that state are old and are ordered to receive him as if he were their hereditary lord.

But let us return to our matter. I say that whoever considers the discourse written above will see that either hatred or disdain has been the cause of the ruin of the emperors named before, and will also know whence it arises that, though some of them proceeded in one mode and some in the contrary mode, in whichever mode, one of them came to a happy end and the others to unhappy ends. For to Pertinax and Alexander, because they were new princes, it was useless and harmful to wish to imitate Marcus, who was in the principate by hereditary right; and similarly, for Caracalla, Commodus, and Maximinus it was a pernicious thing to imitate Severus, because they did not have as much virtue as would allow them to follow in his footsteps. Therefore, a new prince in a new principality cannot imitate the actions of Marcus, nor again is it necessary to follow those of Severus; but he should take from Severus those parts which are necessary to found his state and from Marcus those which are fitting and glorious to conserve a state that is already established and firm.

24. The formal or plural you.

Whether Fortresses and Many Other Things Which Are Made and Done by Princes Every Day Are Useful or Useless

Some princes have disarmed their subjects so as to hold their states securely; some others have kept their subject towns divided; some have nourished enmities against themselves; some others have turned to gaining to themselves those who had been suspect to them at the beginning of their states; some have built fortresses; some have knocked them down and destroyed them. And although one cannot give a definite judgment on all these things unless one comes to the particulars of those states where any such decision has to be made, nonetheless I shall speak in that broad mode which the matter permits in itself.

There has never been, then, a new prince who has disarmed his subjects; on the contrary, whenever he has found them unarmed, he has always armed them. For when they are armed, those arms become yours; those whom you suspected become faithful, and those who were faithful remain so; and from subjects they are made into your partisans. And because all subjects cannot be armed, if those whom you arm are benefited, one can act with more security toward the others. The difference of treatment that they recognize regarding themselves makes them obligated to you; the others excuse you, judging it necessary that those who have more danger and more obligation deserve more. But, when you disarm them, you begin to offend them; you show that you distrust them either for cowardice or for lack of faith, both of which opinions generate hatred against you. And because you cannot remain unarmed, you must turn to a mercenary military, which is of the quality described above;[1] and even if it were good, it cannot be so good as to defend you against powerful enemies and suspect subjects. So, as I said, a new prince of a new principality always has ordered the arms there. The histories are full of examples of this.

But when a prince acquires a new state that is added as a member to his old one, then it is necessary to disarm that state, except for those who were your partisans in acquiring it. These, too, it is necessary to render soft and effeminate, in time and with opportunity, and to be ordered so that the arms of all your state are only with your own soldiers, who live next to you in your old state.

Our ancients, and those who were esteemed wise, used to say that it was necessary to hold Pistoia with parties and Pisa with fortresses; and because of this they nourished differences in some towns subject to them, so as to hold them more easily. In times when Italy was in balance in a certain mode, this would have been good to do, but I do not believe that one could give it today as a teaching. For I do not believe that divisions ever do any good; on the contrary, when the enemy approaches, of necessity divided cities are immediately lost, because the weaker party always joins the external forces and the other will not be able to rule.

The Venetians, moved as I believe by the reasons written above, nourished the Guelf and Ghibelline sects in the cities subject to them. Although the Venetians never let them come to blood, still they nourished these contentions among them, so that occupied as those citizens were with their differences, they did not unite against the Venetians. As may be seen, this did not turn out according to their plan later, because when they were defeated at Vailà, one party immediately became daring, and took all of their state from

1. See Chapter 12.

them. Such modes, therefore, imply weakness in the prince. For in a vigorous principality such divisions are never permitted, because they bring profit only in time of peace, as subjects can be managed more easily through them; but when war comes, such an order shows its own fallaciousness.

Without doubt princes become great when they overcome difficulties made for them and opposition made to them. So fortune, especially when she wants to make a new prince great—since he has a greater necessity to acquire reputation than a hereditary prince—makes enemies arise for him and makes them undertake enterprises against him, so that he has cause to overcome them and to climb higher on the ladder that his enemies have brought for him. Therefore many judge that a wise prince, when he has the opportunity for it, should astutely nourish some enmity so that when he has crushed it, his greatness emerges the more from it.

Princes, and especially those that are new, have found more faith and more utility in those men who at the beginning of their states were held to be suspect than in those whom they trusted at the beginning. Pandolfo Petrucci, prince of Siena, ruled his state more with those who had been suspect to him than with the others. But one cannot speak broadly of this thing because it varies according to the subject. I will only say this, that the prince will always be able to win over to himself with the greatest ease those men who in the beginning of a principality had been enemies, and who are of such quality that to maintain themselves they need somewhere to lean. They are all the more forced to serve him faithfully as they know it is more necessary for them to cancel out with deeds the sinister opinion one has taken of them. And so the prince always extracts more use from them than from those who, while serving him with too much security, neglect his affairs.

And since the matter requires it, I do not want to leave

out a reminder to princes who have newly taken a state through internal support within it, that they consider well what cause moved those who supported them to support them. If it is not natural affection toward them but only because those supporters were not content with that state, he will be able to keep them his friends with trouble and great difficulty, because it is impossible for him to make them content. And while reviewing[2] well the cause of this, with examples drawn from ancient and modern things, he will see that it is much easier to gain as friends to himself men who were content with the state beforehand, and therefore were his enemies, than those who, because they were not content with it, became friends and gave him support in seizing it.

It has been the custom of princes, so as to be able to hold their states more securely, to build fortresses that would be a bridle and bit for those who might plan to act against them, and to have a secure refuge from sudden attack.[3] I praise this mode because it has been used since antiquity. Nonetheless, in our times Messer Niccolò Vitelli was seen to destroy two fortresses in Città di Castello in order to hold that state. When Guidobaldo, duke of Urbino, returned to his dominion from which Cesare Borgia had expelled him, he razed all the fortresses in that province to their foundations; and he judged that without them he would with greater difficulty lose his state again. When the Bentivogli returned to Bologna, they adopted similar measures. Fortresses are thus useful or not according to the times, and if they do well for you in one regard, they hurt[4] you in another. And one may discuss this issue thus. The prince who has more fear of the people than of foreigners ought to make fortresses, but the one who has more fear of

2. lit.: discoursing on.
3. On fortresses, see *Discourses on Livy* II 21, 24, 25; III 27, 37.
4. lit.: offend.

foreigners than of the people, ought to omit them. The castle in Milan built by Francesco Sforza has brought and will bring more war to the Sforza house than any other disorder of that state. Therefore the best fortress there is, is not to be hated by the people, because although you may have fortresses, if the people hold you in hatred fortresses do not save you; for to peoples who have taken up arms foreigners will never be lacking to come to their aid. In our times fortresses have not been seen to bring profit to any prince, unless to the Countess of Forlì, when Count Girolamo, her consort, died; for by means of a fortress she was able to escape a popular uprising,[5] to await help from Milan, and to recover her state.[6] And the times then were such that a foreigner could not help the people. But later, fortresses were worth little to her when Cesare Borgia attacked her, and her hostile people joined with the foreigner. Therefore, then and before it would have been more secure for her not to be hated by the people than to have had fortresses. So, having considered all these things, I shall praise whoever makes fortresses and whoever does not, and I shall blame anyone who, trusting in fortresses, thinks little of being hated by the people.

5. lit.: impetus.
6. This story is told in vivid detail in *Discourses on Livy* III 6 and *Florentine Histories* VIII 34.

❦ XXI ❦

What a Prince Should Do to Be Held in Esteem

Nothing makes a prince so much esteemed as to carry on great enterprises and to give rare examples of himself. In our times we have Ferdinand of Aragon, the present king of Spain. This man can be called an almost new prince because from being a weak king he has become by fame and by glory the first king among the Christians; and, if you consider his actions, you[1] will find them all very great and some of them extraordinary. In the beginning of his reign he attacked Granada, and that enterprise was the foundation of his state. First, he made it at leisure and without fear of being interfered with; he kept the minds of the barons of Castile preoccupied; while thinking of that war, they did not think of innovating. And in the meantime he acquired reputation and power[2] over them which they did not perceive. He was able to sustain armies with money from the Church and the people, and with that long war to lay a foundation for his own military, which later brought him honor. Besides this, in order to undertake greater enterprises, always making use of religion, he turned to an act of pious cruelty, expelling the Marranos from his kingdom and despoiling it of them;[3] nor could there be an example more wretched and rarer than this. He attacked Africa under this same cloak, made his campaign in Italy, and has lately attacked France;[4] and so he has always done and ordered great things, which have always kept the minds of his subjects in suspense and admiration, and occupied with their outcome. And his actions have followed upon one another in such a mode that he has never allowed an interval between them for men to be able to work quietly against him.

It also helps very much for a prince to give rare examples of himself in governing internally, similar to those that

---

1. Both *you*'s in this sentence are the formal or plural you.
2. lit.: empire.
3. The Marranos, who were expelled from Spain in 1501–2 by Ferdinand, were Jews and Moslems who had been forcibly converted to Christianity.
4. In 1512, when Ferdinand joined the Holy League.

are told of Messer Bernabò da Milano,[5] when the opportunity arises of someone who works for something extraordinary in civil life, either for good or for ill, and of picking a mode of rewarding or punishing him of which much will be said. And above all a prince should contrive to give himself the fame of a great man and of an excellent talent[6] in every action of his.

A prince is also esteemed when he is a true friend and a true enemy, that is, when without any hesitation he discloses himself in support of someone against another. This course is always more useful than to remain neutral, because if two powers close to you come to grips, either they are of such quality that if one wins, you have to fear the winner, or not. In either of these two cases, it will always be more useful to you to disclose yourself and to wage open[7] war; for in the first case if you do not disclose yourself, you will always be the prey of whoever wins, to the pleasure and satisfaction of the one who was defeated, and you have no reason, nor anything, to defend you or give you refuge. For whoever wins does not want suspect friends who may not help him in adversity; whoever loses does not give you refuge, since you did not want to share his fortune with arms in hand.

Antiochus came into Greece, summoned there by the Aetolians to expel the Romans from it. Antiochus sent spokesmen to the Achaeans, who were friends of the Romans, to urge them to remain in the middle; and on the other side, the Romans sought to persuade them to take up arms for them. This matter came up for decision in the council of the Achaeans, where the legate from Antiochus was persuading them to remain neutral, to which the Roman legate responded: "As to what they say, moreover,

5. Bernabò Visconti, duke of Milan from 1354 to 1385.
6. Or man, in some MSS.
7. lit.: good.

that you should not intervene in the war, nothing is more alien to your interests; without thanks, without dignity you will be the prize of the victor."[8]

And it will always happen that the one who is not friendly will seek your neutrality, and he who is friendly to you will ask that you declare yourself with arms. And irresolute princes, in order to escape present dangers, follow that neutral way most times, and most times come to ruin. But, when the prince discloses himself boldly in support of one side, if the one to whom you adhere wins, although he is powerful and you remain at his discretion, he has an obligation to you and has a contract of love for you; and men are never so indecent as to crush you with so great an example of ingratitude. Then, too, victories are never so clear that the winner does not have to have some respect, especially for justice. But if the one to whom you adhere loses, you are given refuge by him; and he helps you while he can, and you become the companion of a fortune that can revive. In the second case, when those who fight together are of such quality that you do not have to fear the one who wins, so much the greater is the prudence of joining sides; for you assist in the ruin of one with the aid of the other who ought to save him, if he were wise; and when he has won, he remains at your discretion; and with your aid it is impossible that he not win.

And here it is to be noted that a prince must beware never to associate with someone more powerful than himself so as to attack[9] others, except when necessity presses, as was said above. For when you win, you are left his prisoner, and princes should avoid as much as they can being at the discretion of others. The Venetians accompanied France against the duke of Milan, and they could have avoided being in that company—from which their ruin resulted.

8. Quoted in Latin from Livy, *Histories,* XXXV. 49.
9. lit.: offend.

But when one cannot avoid it (as happened to the Florentines when the pope and Spain went with their armies to attack Lombardy), then the prince should join for the reasons given above. Nor should any state ever believe that it can always adopt safe courses; on the contrary, it should think it has to take them all as doubtful. For in the order of things it is found that one never seeks to avoid one inconvenience without running into another; but prudence consists in knowing how to recognize the qualities of inconveniences, and in picking the less bad as good.

A prince should also show himself a lover of the virtues, giving recognition to virtuous men, and he should honor those who are excellent in an art. Next, he should inspire his citizens to follow their pursuits quietly, in trade and in agriculture and in every other pursuit of men, so that one person does not fear to adorn his possessions for fear that they be taken away from him, and another to open up a trade for fear of taxes. But he should prepare rewards for whoever wants to do these things, and for anyone who thinks up any way of expanding his city or his state. Besides this, he should at suitable times of the year keep the people occupied with festivals and spectacles. And because every city is divided into guilds or into clans, he should take account of those communities,[10] meet with them sometimes, and make himself an example of humanity and munificence, always holding firm the majesty of his dignity nonetheless, because he can never want this to be lacking in anything.

10. See Chapter 19, note 12.

❧ XXII ❧

Of Those Whom Princes Have as Secretaries

The choice of ministers is of no small importance to a prince; they are good or not according to the prudence of the prince. And the first conjecture that is to be made of the brain of a lord is to see the men he has around him; and when they are capable and faithful, he can always be reputed wise because he has known how to recognize them as capable and to maintain them as faithful. But if they are otherwise, one can always pass unfavorable judgment on him, because the first error he makes, he makes in this choice.

There was no one who knew Messer Antonio da Venafro[1] as minister of Pandolfo Petrucci, prince of Siena,[2] who did not judge Pandolfo to be a most worthy man, since he had Antonio as his minister. And since there are three kinds of brains: one that understands by itself, another that discerns what others understand, the third that understands neither by itself nor through others; the first is most excellent, the second excellent, and the third useless—it follows, therefore, of necessity that, if Pandolfo was not in the first rank, he was in the second. For every time that one has the judgment to recognize the good or evil that someone does or says, although he does not have the inventiveness by himself, he knows the bad deeds and the good of his minister and extols[3] the one and corrects the other; and the minister cannot hope to deceive him and remains good himself.

---

1. Antonio Giordani da Venafro (1459–1530), professor of law at the Studio of Siena.

2. This is the second time Petrucci has been called "prince of Siena" (cf. Chapter 20); in *Discourses on Livy* III 6 he is called "tyrant of Siena."

3. lit.: exalts.

But as to how a prince can know his minister, here is a mode that never fails. When you see a minister thinking more of himself than of you, and in all actions looking for something useful to himself, one so made will never be a good minister; never will you be able to trust him, because he who has someone's state in his hands should never think of himself but always of the prince, and he should never remember anything that does not pertain to the prince. And on the other side, the prince should think of the minister so as to keep him good—honoring him, making him rich, obligating him to himself, sharing honors and burdens with him so that he sees he cannot stand without the prince and so that many honors do not make him desire more honors, much wealth does not make him desire more wealth, and many burdens make him fear changes. When, therefore, ministers and princes in relation to ministers are so constituted, they can trust one another; when it is otherwise, the end is always damaging either for one or the other.

❧ XXIII ❧

In What Mode Flatterers Are to Be Avoided

I do not want to leave out an important point and an error from which princes defend themselves with difficulty, unless they are very prudent or make good choices. And these are the flatterers of whom courts are full; for men take such pleasure in their own affairs and so deceive themselves there that they defend themselves with difficulty from this plague, and in trying to defend oneself from it one risks the danger of becoming contemptible. For there is no other way to guard oneself from flattery unless men understand that they do not offend you in telling you the truth; but when everyone can tell you the truth, they lack reverence for you. Therefore, a prudent prince must hold to a third mode, choosing wise men in his state; and only to these should he give freedom[1] to speak the truth to him, and of those things only that he asks about and nothing else. But he should ask them about everything and listen to their opinions; then he should decide by himself, in his own mode; and with these councils and with each member of them he should behave in such a mode that everyone knows that the more freely he speaks, the more he will be accepted. Aside from these, he should not want to hear anyone; he should move directly to the thing that was decided and be obstinate in his decisions. Whoever does otherwise either falls headlong because of flatterers or changes often because of the variability of views, from which a low estimation of him arises.

I want to bring up a modern example in this regard. Father Luca, a man of the present emperor Maximilian,[2] speaking of his majesty, told how he did not take counsel from anyone and never did anything in his own mode; this arose from holding to a policy contrary to that given above. For the emperor is a secretive man who does not communicate his plans to anyone, nor seek their views; but as in putting them into effect they begin to be known and disclosed, they begin to be contradicted by those whom he has around him, and he, an agreeable[3] person, is dissuaded from them.[4] From this it arises that the things he does on one day he destroys on another, that no one ever understands what

1. lit.: free will.
2. Luca Rinaldi, a bishop and ambassador of Emperor Maximilian I (1459–1519), with whom NM became acquainted during his embassy to the emperor in 1508.
3. lit.: easy; see Chapter 15.
4. See NM's similar description of Maximilian, in his *Rapporto delle cose della Magna* (1508).

he wants or plans to do, and that one cannot found oneself on his decisions.

A prince, therefore, should always take counsel, but when he wants, and not when others want it; on the contrary, he should discourage everyone from counseling him about anything unless he asks it of them. But he should be a very broad questioner, and then, in regard to the things he asked about, a patient listener to the truth; indeed, he should become upset when he learns that anyone has any hesitation to speak it to him. And since many esteem that any prince who establishes an opinion of himself as prudent is so considered not because of his nature but because of the good counsel he has around him, without doubt they are deceived. For this is a general rule that never fails: that a prince who is not wise by himself cannot be counseled well, unless indeed by chance he should submit himself to one alone to govern him in everything, who is a very prudent man. In this case he could well be, but it would not last long because that governor would in a short time take away his state. But by taking counsel from more than one, a prince who is not wise will never have united counsel, nor know by himself how to unite them. Each one of his counselors will think of his own interest; he will not know how to correct them or understand them. And they cannot be found otherwise, because men will always turn out bad for you unless they have been made good by a necessity. So one concludes that good counsel, from wherever it comes, must arise from the prudence of the prince, and not the prudence of the prince from good counsel.

❧ XXIV ☙

Why the Princes of Italy Have Lost
Their States

When the things written above have been observed prudently, they make a new prince appear ancient and immediately render him more secure and steady in his state than if he had grown old in it. For a new prince is observed much more in his actions than a hereditary one; and when they are recognized as virtuous, they take hold of men much more and obligate them much more than ancient blood. For men are much more taken by present things than by past ones, and when they find good in the present, they enjoy it and do not seek elsewhere; indeed they will take up every defense on behalf of a new prince if he is not lacking in other things as regards himself. And so he will have the double glory of having made the beginning of a new principality, of having adorned it and consolidated it with good laws, good arms, good friends,[1] and good examples, just as he has a double shame who, having been born prince, has lost it through his lack of prudence.

And if one considers those lords in Italy who have lost their states in our times, like the king of Naples,[2] the duke of Milan,[3] and others, one will find in them, first, a common defect as to arms, the causes of which have been discussed at length above; then, one will see that some of them either had a hostile people or if they had friendly peoples, did not know how to secure themselves against the great. For without these defects, states that have enough nerve to put an

---

1. Most MSS omit "good friends."
2. Frederick of Aragon, expelled from Naples in 1501 by Ferdinand the Catholic and Louis XII, and dethroned.
3. Ludovico Sforza; see Chapter 3.

army into the field are not lost. Philip of Macedon, not the father of Alexander but the one who was defeated by Titus Quintius,[4] did not have much of a state with respect to the greatness of the Romans and of Greece, who attacked him; nonetheless, because he was a military man and knew how to deal with the people and secure himself against the great, he kept up a war against them for many years; and if at the end he lost dominion over several cities, his kingdom remained to him nonetheless.

Therefore, these princes of ours who have been in their principalities for many years may not accuse fortune when they have lost them afterwards, but their own indolence; for, never having thought that quiet times could change (which is a common defect of men, not to take account of the storm during the calm), when later the times became adverse, they thought of fleeing and not of defending themselves. And they hoped that their peoples, disgusted with the insolence of the victors, would call them back. This course is good when others are lacking; but it is indeed bad to have put aside other remedies for this one. For one should never fall in the belief you can find someone to pick you up. Whether it does not happen or happens, it is not security for you, because that defense was base and did not depend on you. And those defenses alone are good, are certain, and are lasting, that depend on you yourself and on your virtue.

4. On Philip V of Macedonia (237–179 B.C.), see *Discourses on Livy* II 4, 10; III 10, 37.

How Much Fortune Can Do in Human Affairs, and in What Mode It May Be Opposed

It is not unknown to me that many have held and hold the opinion that worldly things are so governed by fortune and by God, that men cannot correct them with their prudence, indeed that they have no remedy at all; and on account of this they might judge that one need not sweat much over things but let oneself be governed by chance. This opinion has been believed more in our times because of the great variability of things which have been seen and are seen every day, beyond every human conjecture. When I have thought about this sometimes, I have been in some part inclined to their opinion. Nonetheless, so that our free will not be eliminated, I judge that it might be true that fortune is arbiter of half of our actions, but also that she leaves the other half, or close to it, for us to govern. And I liken her to one of these violent rivers which, when they become enraged, flood the plains, ruin the trees and the buildings, lift earth from this part, drop in another; each person flees before them, everyone yields to their impetus without being able to hinder them in any regard. And although they are like this, it is not as if men, when times are quiet, could not provide for them with dikes and dams so that when they rise later, either they go by a canal or their impetus is neither so wanton nor so damaging. It happens similarly with fortune, which demonstrates her power where virtue has not been put in order[1] to resist her and therefore turns her impetus where she knows that dams and dikes

1. lit.: ordered.

have not been made to contain her. And if you consider Italy, which is the seat of these variations and that which has given them motion, you will see[2] a country without dams and without any dike. If it had been diked by suitable virtue, like Germany, Spain, and France, either this flood would not have brought the great variations that it has, or it would not have come here.

And I wish that this may be enough to have said about opposing fortune in general.[3] But restricting myself more to particulars, I say that one sees a given prince be happy today and come to ruin tomorrow without having seen him change his nature or any quality. This I believe arises, first, from the causes that have been discussed at length in the preceding, that is, that the prince who leans entirely on his fortune comes to ruin as it varies. I believe, further, that he is happy who adapts his mode of proceeding to the qualities of the times; and similarly, he is unhappy whose procedure is in disaccord with the times. For one sees that in the things that lead men to the end that each has before him, that is, glories and riches, they proceed variously: one with caution,[4] the other with impetuosity; one by violence, the other with art; one with patience, the other with its contrary—and with these different modes each can attain it. One also sees two cautious persons, one attaining his plan, the other not; and similarly two persons are equally happy with two different methods, one being cautious, the other impetuous. This arises from nothing other than from the quality of the times that they conform to or not in their procedure. From this follows what I said, that two persons working differently come out with the same effect; and of two persons working identically, one is led to his end, the

2. Both *you*'s in this sentence are the formal or plural you.
3. lit.: universal.
4. lit.: respect; *respetto* is translated usually as "caution" and "hesitation," occasionally as "regard."

other not. On this also depends the variability of the good: for if one governs himself with caution and patience, and the times and affairs turn in such a way that his government is good, he comes out happy; but if the times and affairs change, he is ruined because he does not change his mode of proceeding. Nor may a man be found so prudent as to know how to accommodate himself to this, whether because he cannot deviate from what nature inclines him to or also because, when one has always flourished by walking on one path, he cannot be persuaded to depart from it. And so the cautious man, when it is time to come to impetuosity, does not know how to do it, hence comes to ruin: for if he would change his nature with the times and with affairs, his fortune would not change.

Pope Julius II proceeded impetuously in all his affairs, and he found the times and affairs so much in conformity with his mode of proceeding that he always achieved a happy end. Consider[5] the first enterprise that he undertook in Bologna, while Messer Giovanni Bentivoglio was still living. The Venetians were not content with it; nor was the king of Spain; with France he was holding discussions[6] on that enterprise; and nonetheless, with his ferocity and impetuosity, he personally put that expedition into motion. This move made Spain and the Venetians stand still in suspense, the latter out of fear and the other because of the desire he had to recover the whole kingdom of Naples. From the other side he pulled the king of France after him; because when that king saw him move, and since he desired to make Julius his friend in order to bring down the Venetians, he judged he could not deny him his troops without injuring him openly. Julius thus accomplished with his impetuous move what no other pontiff, with all human prudence, would ever have accomplished, because if he had

5. The formal or plural you should be understood here.
6. lit.: reasonings.

waited to depart from Rome with firm conclusions and everything in order, as any other pontiff would have done, he would never have succeeded. For the king of France would have had a thousand excuses and the others would have raised in him a thousand fears. I wish to omit all his other actions, since all have been alike and all succeeded well. And the brevity of his life did not allow him to feel the contrary, because if times had come when he had needed to proceed with caution, his ruin would have followed: he would never have deviated from those modes to which nature inclined him.[7]

I conclude, thus, that when fortune varies and men remain obstinate in their modes, men are happy while they are in accord, and as they come into discord, unhappy. I judge this indeed, that it is better to be impetuous than cautious, because fortune is a woman; and it is necessary, if one wants to hold her down, to beat her and strike her down. And one sees that she lets herself be won more by the impetuous than by those who proceed coldly. And so always, like a woman, she is the friend of the young, because they are less cautious, more ferocious, and command her with more audacity.

7. See *Discourses on Livy* III 9.

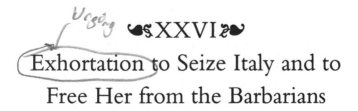

◆§ XXVI ◆◆

Exhortation to Seize Italy and to Free Her from the Barbarians

Thus, having considered everything discussed above, and thinking to myself whether in Italy at present the times have been tending to the honor of a new prince, and whether there is matter to give opportunity to someone prudent and virtuous to introduce a form that would bring honor to him and good to the community of men there, it appears to me that so many things are tending to the benefit of a new prince that I do not know what time has ever been more apt for it. And if, as I said,[1] it was necessary for anyone wanting to see the virtue of Moses that the people of Israel be enslaved in Egypt, and to learn the greatness of spirit of Cyrus, that the Persians be oppressed by the Medes, and to learn the excellence of Theseus, that the Athenians be dispersed, so at present to know the virtue of an Italian spirit[2] it was necessary that Italy be reduced to the condition in which she is at present, which is more enslaved than the Hebrews, more servile than the Persians, more dispersed than the Athenians, without a head, without order, beaten, despoiled, torn, pillaged, and having endured ruin of every sort.

And although up to now a glimmer has shone in someone who could judge that he had been ordered by God for her redemption, yet later it was seen that in the highest course of his actions, he was repulsed by fortune. So, left as if lifeless, she awaits whoever it can be that will heal her wounds, and put an end to the sacking of Lombardy, to the taxes on the kingdom and on Tuscany, and cure her of her sores that have festered now for a long time. One may see how she prays God to send her someone to redeem her from these barbarous cruelties and insults. One may also see her ready and disposed to follow a flag, provided that there be someone to pick it up. Nor may one see at present anyone in whom she can hope more than in your illustrious house, which with its fortune and virtue, supported by God and by the Church of which it is now prince,[3] can put itself at the

1. See Chapter 6.
2. *spirito,* not *animo.*
3. Cardinal Giovanni de' Medici, Lorenzo's uncle, became Pope Leo X in 1513.

head of this redemption. This is not very difficult if you[4] summon up the actions and lives of those named above. And although these men are rare and marvelous, nonetheless they were men, and each of them had less opportunity than the present; for their undertaking was not more just than this one, nor easier, nor was God more friendly to them than to you. Here there is great justice: "for war is just to whom it is necessary, and arms are pious when there is no hope but in arms."[5] Here there is very great readiness, and where there is great readiness, there cannot be great difficulty, provided that your house keeps its aim on the orders of those whom I have put forth. Besides this, here may be seen extraordinary things without example, brought about[6] by God: the sea has opened; a cloud has escorted you along the way; the stone has poured forth water; here manna has rained;[7] everything has concurred in your greatness. The remainder you must do yourself. God does not want to do everything, so as not to take free will from us and that part of the glory that falls to us.

And it is not a marvel if none of the Italians named before has been able to do what it is hoped will be done by your illustrious house, and if in so many revolutions in Italy and in so many maneuvers of war, it always appears that military virtue has died out in her. This arises from the fact that her ancient orders were not good, and that there has not been anyone who has known how to find new ones; and nothing brings so much honor to a man rising newly as the

4. The formal or plural you.

5. Quoted in Latin from Livy IX. 1; see also *Discourses on Livy* III 12, and *Florentine Histories* V 8, where the same quotation is used to emphasize necessity rather than justice.

6. lit.: conducted.

7. These are references to miracles that occurred as Moses led the Israelites to the promised land, just before the revelation at Mount Sinai. They are not given in the same order as in the Bible, Exodus 14:21, 13:21, 17:6, 16:4.

new laws and the new orders found by him. When these things have been founded well and have greatness in them, they make him revered and admirable. And in Italy matter is not lacking for introducing every form; here there is great virtue in the limbs, if it were not lacking in the heads. Look how in duels and in encounters with few the Italians are superior in force, dexterity, and ingenuity. But when it comes to armies, they do not compare. And everything follows from the weakness at the head, because those who know are not obeyed, and each thinks he knows, since up to now no one has been able to raise himself, both by virtue and by fortune, to a point where the others will yield to him. From this it follows that in so much time, in so many wars made in the last twenty years, when there has been an army entirely Italian it has always proven to be bad. The first testimony to this is Taro, then Alessandria, Capua, Genoa, Vailà, Bologna, Mestre.[8]

Thus, if your illustrious house wants to follow those excellent men who redeemed their countries,[9] it is necessary before all other things, as the true foundation of every undertaking, to provide itself with its own arms; for one cannot have more faithful, nor truer, nor better soldiers. And although each of them may be good, all together become better when they see themselves commanded by their prince, and honored and indulged by him. It is necessary, therefore, to prepare such arms for oneself so as to be able with Italian virtue to defend oneself from foreigners. And although Swiss and Spanish infantry are esteemed to be terrifying, nonetheless there is a defect in both, by means of which a third order might not only oppose them but also be confident of overcoming them. For the Spanish cannot withstand horse, and the Swiss have to be afraid of infantry if they meet in combat any that are obstinate like themselves. Hence it has been seen, and will be seen by experi-

8. Seven battles that were Italian defeats, from 1495 to 1513.
9. lit.: provinces.

ence, that the Spanish cannot withstand French cavalry, and the Swiss are ruined by Spanish infantry. And although a complete experiment of this last has not been seen, yet an indication of it was seen in the battle of Ravenna,[10] when the Spanish infantry confronted the German battalions, who use the same order as the Swiss. There the Spanish, with their agile bodies and aided by their bucklers, came between and under the Germans' pikes and attacked them safely without their having any remedy for it; and if it had not been for the cavalry that charged them, they would have worn out all the Germans. Having thus learned the defects of both of these infantry, one can order a new one that would resist horse and not be afraid of infantry; this will be done by a regeneration of arms and a change in orders. And these are among those things which, when newly ordered, give reputation and greatness to a new prince.

Thus, one should not let this opportunity pass, for Italy, after so much time, to see her redeemer. I cannot express with what love he would be received in all those provinces that have suffered from these floods from outside; with what thirst for revenge, with what obstinate faith, with what piety, with what tears. What doors would be closed to him? What peoples would deny him obedience? What envy would oppose him? What Italian would deny him homage? This barbarian domination stinks to everyone. Then may your illustrious house take up this task with the spirit and hope in which just enterprises are taken up, so that under its emblem this fatherland may be ennobled and under its auspices the saying of Petrarch's may come true:

> Virtue will take up arms against fury,
> and make the battle short,
> because the ancient valor in Italian hearts
> is not yet dead.[11]

10. April 11, 1512; see Chapter 3.
11. Petrarch, *Italia mia,* 93–96.

Appendix

In the following letter, which has been called the most celebrated in all of Italian literature, Machiavelli describes one day in his life and remarks casually that he has just completed *The Prince*. The letter was written in response to his friend Francesco Vettori, Florentine ambassador in Rome, who had previously sent a letter describing a day in *his* life. Machiavelli's reply is partly a parody of Vettori's somewhat self-important recounting, but it also gives us a glimpse, from the outside, of the political philosopher at work. We learn, among other things, that *The Prince* arose from conversations with the ancients, and that, in it, Machiavelli delved as deeply as he could into his subject.

NICCOLÒ MACHIAVELLI TO FRANCESCO VETTORI, FLORENCE, DECEMBER 10, 1513.

Magnificent ambassador:

"Never were divine favors late."[1] I say this because I appear to have lost, no, mislaid your favor, since you have gone a long time without writing me, and I was doubtful whence the cause could arise. And of all those that came to my mind I took little account except for one, when I feared you had stopped writing to me because someone had written to you that I was not a good warden of your letters; and I knew that, apart from Filippo and Pagolo, no one else had seen them on account of me. I regained your favor by your last letter of the 23rd of last month, where I was very pleased to see how orderly and quietly you exercise this public office; and I urge you to continue so, for whoever lets go of his own convenience for the convenience of others, only loses his own and gets no thanks from them. And because Fortune wants to do everything, she wants us to allow her to do it, to remain quiet and not give trouble, and to await the

---

1. Petrarch, *Triumph of Divinity*, 13.

time at which she allows men something to do; and then it will be right for you to give more effort, to watch things more, and for me to leave my villa and say: "Here I am." Therefore, wishing to return equal favors, I cannot tell you in this letter of mine anything other than what my life is like, and if you judge that it should be bartered for yours, I will be content to exchange it.

I stay in my villa, and since these last chance events occurred,[2] I have not spent, to add them all up, twenty days in Florence. Until now I have been catching thrushes with my own hands. I would get up before day, prepare traps, and go out with a bundle of cages on my back, so that I looked like Geta when he returned from the harbor with Amphitryon's books; I caught at least two, at most six thrushes. And so passed all September; then this pastime, though annoying and strange, gave out, to my displeasure. And what my life is like, I will tell you. I get up in the morning with the sun and go to a wood of mine that I am having cut down, where I stay for two hours to look over the work of the past day, and to pass time with the wood-cutters, who always have some disaster on their hands either among themselves or with their neighbors. And regarding this wood I would have a thousand beautiful things to tell you of what happened to me with Frosino da Panzano and others who want wood from it. And Frosino in particular sent for a number of loads without telling me anything, and on payment wanted to hold back ten lire from me, which he said he should have had from me four years ago when he beat me at *cricca* at Antonio Guicciardini's. I began to raise the devil and was on the point of accusing the driver who had gone for it of theft; but Giovanni Machiavelli came between us and brought us to agree. Batista Guicciardini, Filippo Ginori, Tommaso del Bene,

2. Perhaps a reference to NM's imprisonment and torture in February and March of 1513.

and some other citizens, when that north wind was blowing, ordered a load each from me. I promised to all, and sent one to Tommaso which in Florence turned into a half-load, because to stack it up there were himself, his wife, his servant, and his children, so that they looked like Gabbura with his boys when he bludgeons an ox on Thursday. So, when I saw whose profit it was, I told the others I had no more wood; and all have made a big point of it, especially Batista, who counts this among the other disasters of Prato.

When I leave the wood, I go to a spring, and from there to an aviary of mine. I have a book under my arm, Dante or Petrarch, or one of the minor poets like Tibullus, Ovid, and such. I read of their amorous passions and their loves; I remember my own and enjoy myself for a while in this thinking. Then I move on along the road to the inn; I speak with those passing by; I ask them news of their places; I learn various things; and I note the various tastes and different fancies of men. In the meantime comes the hour to dine, when I eat with my company what food this poor villa and tiny patrimony allow. Having eaten, I return to the inn; there is the host, ordinarily a butcher, a miller, two bakers. With them I become a rascal for the whole day, playing at *cricca* and *tric-trac*, from which arise a thousand quarrels and countless abuses with insulting words, and most times we are fighting over a penny and yet we can be heard shouting from San Casciano. Thus involved with these vermin I scrape the mold off my brain and I satisfy the malignity of this fate of mine, as I am content to be trampled on this path so as to see if she will be ashamed of it.

When evening has come, I return to my house and go into my study. At the door I take off my clothes of the day, covered with mud and mire, and I put on my regal and courtly garments; and decently reclothed, I enter the ancient courts of ancient men, where, received by them lovingly, I feed on the food that alone is mine and that I was born for. There I am not ashamed to speak with them and to ask them the reason for their actions; and they in their humanity reply to me. And for the space of four hours I feel no boredom, I forget every pain, I do not fear poverty, death does not frighten me. I deliver myself entirely to them. And because Dante says that to have understood without retaining does not make knowledge,[3] I have noted what capital I have made from their conversation and have composed a little work *De Principatibus* [On Principalities], where I delve as deeply as I can into reflections on this subject, debating what a principality is, of what kinds they are, how they are acquired, how they are maintained, why they are lost. And if you have ever been pleased by any of my whimsies, this one should not displease you; and to a prince, and especially to a new prince, it should be welcome. So I am addressing it to his Magnificence, Giuliano.[4] Filippo Casavecchia has seen it; he can give you an account in part both of the thing in itself and of the discussions I had with him, although I am all the time fattening and polishing it.

You wish, magnificent ambassador, that I leave this life and come to enjoy your life with you. I will do it in any case, but what tempts me now is certain dealings of mine which I will have done in six weeks. What makes me be doubtful is that the Soderini are there, whom I would be forced, if I came, to visit and speak with. I should fear that at my return I would not expect to get off at my house, but I would get off at the Bargello,[5] for although this state has very great foundations and great security, yet it is new, and because of this suspicious; nor does it lack wiseacres who, to

3. *Paradiso*, V, 41–42.

4. Giuliano de' Medici, the duke of Nemours, son of Lorenzo the Magnificent. He left Florence in September of 1513 and was in Rome at the time of NM's letter. He died in 1516, and NM decided to dedicate *The Prince* to Lorenzo de' Medici, grandson of Lorenzo the Magnificent, who became duke of Urbino in 1516.

5. The prison, because NM would be suspected of plotting with the Soderini for the return of the previous regime.

appear like Pagolo Bertini, would let others run up a bill and leave me to think of paying. I beg you to relieve me of this fear, and then I will come in the time stated to meet you anyway.

I have discussed with Filippo this little work of mine, whether to give it to him[6] or not; and if it is good to give it, whether it would be good for me to take it or send it to you. Not giving it would make me fear that at the least it would not be read by Giuliano and that this Ardinghelli would take for himself the honor of this latest effort of mine. The necessity that chases me makes me give it, because I am becoming worn out, and I cannot remain as I am for a long time without becoming despised because of poverty, besides the desire I have that these Medici lords begin to make use of me even if they should begin by making me roll a stone. For if I should not then win them over to me, I should complain of myself; and through this thing, if it were read, one would see that I have neither slept through nor played away the fifteen years I have been at the study of the art of the state. And anyone should be glad to have the service of one who is full of experience at the expense of another. And one should not doubt my faith, because having always observed faith, I ought not now be learning to break it. Whoever has been faithful and good for forty-three years, as I have, ought not to be able to change his nature, and of my faith and goodness my poverty is witness.

I should like, then, for you to write me again on how this matter appears to you, and I commend myself to you.

Be prosperous.

10 December 1513

Niccolò Machiavelli, in Florence.

6. Giuliano.

Glossary

English terms appearing in the translation are in boldface, followed by the Italian or Latin terms they translate in italics and the listing of their occurrences by chapter and page number. Certain abbreviations are slightly different from those used in the introduction and the notes to the text: ED refers to the dedicatory letter, and T to a chapter title. A parenthetical number followed by a multiplication cross (✕) indicates multiple occurrences. (L) indicates a Latin word. Negatives and other words with prefixes are listed with their root words. Indicators of parts of speech (n. for noun, v. for verb, adj. for adjective) are given only where the English terms are identical. *See also* refers to another English term used to translate that Italian word; *cf.* refers to an etymologically or conceptually related term.

An asterisk next to an English or Italian term indicates that not ?ll occurrences of that term are listed in the glossary; all occurrences are given for other listed English terms (when they translate Italian, not necessarily Latin) and for listed Italian terms (though it may be necessary to consult the entries cross-referenced under *See also* to locate all occurrences of a listed Italian term). Occurrences of English terms when they translate Latin are usually given only when the Latin terms are cognates of the Italian term translated. The glossary does not include words inserted in the translation in brackets for clarification.

abject, *abietta,* 8.34

absolute, *assoluto,* 9.42 (2✕)

accident, *accidente,* 2.6, 3.11, 5.21, 8.38, 14.60

account,* *conto,* 10.43, 18.69, 19.72 (2✕), 19.74, 21.91, 24.97

accuse, *accusare,* 7.33, 24.97. *Cf.* excuse

accustom, *assuefare,* 2.6, 13.57, 14.59; **accustom,** *consueto,* 1.6, 5.20, 5.21; **accustom,** *solere,** 9.42. For *solere, see also* custom

acquire, acquisition, *acquistare, acquisto, acquistato, acquiruntur* (L), ED.3, 1.5 (T), 1.5, 1.6 (2✕), 3.8 (2✕), 3.9 (5✕), 3.10, 3.11 (3✕), 3.13, 3.14 (2✕), 4.16, 4.17, 4.19, 5.20, 6.21 (T), 6.22 (2✕), 6.23 (2✕), 6.25, 7.25 (T), 7.26, 7.27, 7.28 (3✕), 8.35, 8.36, 11.45, 12.48, 12.52 (3✕), 13.55, 14.58, 16.64, 17.66, 17.67, 19.77, 20.84 (2✕), 20.85, 21.88; **reacquire,** *riacquistare,* 2.7. *Cf.* gain

action, *azione,* ED.3, 6.22 (2✕), 6.23, 7.27, 7.32, 7.33, 8.35, 11.47, 13.55, 14.60 (2✕), 17.67 (3✕), 18.71, 19.72, 19.75, 19.78,

19.79, 19.82, 21.88 (2×), 21.89, 22.93, 24.96, 25.98, 25.101, 26.102, 26.103

adequate, *iusto,* 10.43. *See also* just

administer, *sumministrare,* 16.64, 19.75; *administrare* (L), 5.20 (T); **administrator,** *amministratore,* 4.17; **administration,** *amministrazione,* 19.76, 19.81

advantage, *vantaggio,* 3.12, 14.59 (2×); **advantage,** *commodità,* 19.73; **disadvantage,** *disavvantagio,* 3.15. *Cf.* convenience

advocate (n.), *avvocato,* 7.30

afraid, *avere paura,* 7.33, 26.104, 26.105; *pauroso,* 3.10. *See also* fear

alive, *vivo,* 7.32

alone, *solo,*★ 3.12, 9.39, 11.45, 19.73; *solamente,* 24.97; **one alone,** *uno solo,* 23.95

ambition, *ambizione,* 3.11, 3.13, 4.17, 11.47, 12.51 (2×), 19.72, 19.74–75, 19.76; **ambitious,** *ambizioso,* 3.14 (2×), 9.40, 12.48

ancient, *antiquo, antico, antiquato,* ED.3, 2.7, 3.9 (3×), 4.17, 5.21 (2×), 8.34, 12.50, 13.54, 18.69 (2×), 19.82, 20.84, 20.86, 24.96 (2×), 26.103, 26.105. For *antiquo, antico, see also* antiquity; former; old

anticipation, *sospetto,* 19.73. *See also* suspect

antiquity, *antiquità,* 2.7, 4.17; **since antiquity,** *ad antiquo,* 20.86. For *antiquo, see also* ancient; former; old

appetite, *appetito,* 9.39 (2×)

arbiter, *arbitro,* 3.11, 3.14, 12.53, 25.98. *Cf.* free; liberty; will

arm★ (n.), *arma, armi, arme, arma* (L), ED.3, 1.6, 3.8, 5.21, 6.21 (T), 7.25 (T), 7.27 (3×), 7.28 (3×), 7.30 (2×), 7.32, 11.46 (2×), 11.47, 12.48 (6×), 12.49 (5×), 12.50 (5×), 12.52 (4×), 12.53, 13.54 (6×), 13.55 (7×), 13.56 (7×), 13.57 (3×),14.58 (2×), 19.72 (2×), 20.83 (2×), 20.84 (2×), 20.87, 21.89 (2×), 21.90, 24.96 (2×), 26.103 (2×) (L), 26.104 (2×), 26.105 (2×); *braccio,* 7.29; **men–at–arms,** *gente d'armi, gente d'arme, genti d'arme,* 3.8, 3.10, 3.11, 13.56 (2×); **arm** (v.), **armed,** *armare, armato, armo* (L), 6.24, 7.30, 12.50 (4×), 12.51, 13.56 (2×), 13.57, 14.58 (4×), 20.83 (3×); **disarm,** *disarmare,* 20.83 (3×), 20.84; **disarmed,** *disarmato* (adj.), 6.24 (2×), 12.50, 20.83; **unarmed,** *disarmato,* 13.54, 14.58 (4×), 20.83, 20.84; **very well armed,** *armatissimo,* 12.50

army, *esercito,* 3.8, 3.9, 3.11, 4.18, 7.31, 7.32, 8.34, 9.41, 10.43, 10.44, 12.53, 13.54, 13.56(2×), 14.59(3×), 14.60(2×), 16.64(2×), 17.67(3×), 17.68, 19.77, 19.78(3×), 19.79(3×), 19.80(2×), 19.81(3×), 21.88, 21.91, 24.97, 26.101, 26.104

arrangements, *governi,* 7.30. *See also* govern
art, *arte,* 9.40, 14.58(4×), 19.76, 21.91, 25.99. *See also* cunning
artillery, *artiglieria,* 10.43
assert, *asseverare,* 18.70
associate, *fare compagnia,* 21.90
astonish, *attonito,* 19.78
astuteness, astutely, astute, *astuzia,* 9.39, 9.40, 18.68, 18.69, 20.85;
    astute, *astuto,* 15.62; **very astute,** *astutissima,* 19.79
attack,* *offendere,* 7.30, 21.90, 26.05. *See also* hurt; offend
auspices, *auspizii,* 26.105
authority, *autorità,* 3.11, 3.14, 4.17, 4.19, 7.30, 9.39, 9.42, 13.55,
    19.74, 19.82
avarice, *avarizia,* 19.76 (2×); *avaro,* untranslated, 15.61. *Cf.* revenge
avenge, *vendicare, vendicarsi,* 3.10, 17.68, 19.78
bad, *cattivo,* 17.67; **bad, badly,** *malo, male,* 7.33, 8.37, 8.38 (3×),
    13.54, 17.65, 24.97, 26.104; *tristo,* 19.77 (2×), 19.78, 21.91,
    22.92, 23.95. For *mal contento, see also* content; for *male, see also*
    evil; ill; for *mal resoluto, see also* irresolute. *Cf.* malignity
barbarian, *barbaro, barbarus* (L), 26.101 (T), 26.102, 26.105
base, *vile,* 24.97; **very base,** *vilissimo,* 19.80 (2×); **baseness,** *viltà,*
    19.81; **debase,** *invilire,* 13.56. *See also* cowardice
battalion, *battaglia,* 26.105
battle, *giornata,* 10.43, 14.59, 26.105; **battle,** *zuffa,* 12.53; **battle,**
    el combatter[e], 26.105. For *giornata, see also* day; for *combattere,*
    see also combat; fight
beast, *bestia,* 18.69 (4×); **bestial,** *bestiale,* 19.80
beg, *pregare,* 6.24, 8.36. *See also* pray
beginning (n.), *principio,* 3.12 (2×), 8.38, 12.48, 12.51, 13.55, 13.57,
    19.77, 19.78, 20.83, 20.85 (3×), 21.88, 24.96
believe, *credere,* 3.8, 6.23–24, 6.24 (5×), 7.33, 8.37, 9.40, 12.49,
    17.66, 19.73 (3×), 20.84 (3×), 21.91, 24.97, 25.98, 25.99 (2×);
    belief, *credenza,* 3.8; **unbeliever,** *discredente,* 6.24; **unbelieving,**
    incredulo, 15.62; **incredulity,** *incredulità,* 6.23. *Cf.* credit; opinion;
    reputation; trust
belongings, *suppellettile,* ED.3. *Cf.* property
benefit,* *benefizio,* 3.13, 5.21, 7.33, 8.38, 10.44, 19.79, 26.102; *benifi-*
    care, 7.33, 8.38, 20.83; **benefactor,** *beneficatore,* 9.40
bit, *freno,* 19.75, 20.86. For *freno, see also* check; *cf.* bridle
blame (n.), *biasimo,* 3.15 (2×), 15.61; **blame** (v.), *biasimare, biasimato,*

3.13, 3.14, 20.87; **blamed,** *vituperant(ur)* (L), 15.61 (T); **blame, blameable,** *carico,* 19.75 (3×). *See also* burden; *cf.* insult

blood, *sangue,* 17.66, 19.81, 20.84, 24.96; **bloodline,** *sangue,* 1.5, 2.6, 3.9, 4.17, 4.18 (2×), 4.19, 5.21, 7.30; **bloody,** *sanguinoso,* 7.30. For *sangue, see also* life

body, *corpo,* 3.9, 8.34, 13.55, 14.59, 19.80, 26.105

born, *nascere,* 7.26, 8.34, 14.58, 19.74, 24.96

bought, *meritare,* 17.66. *See also* deserve, worthy

brain, *cervello,* 18.69, 22.92 (2×)

bridle, *briglia,* 20.86. *Cf.* bit, check

bring up, *addurre,* 6.22, 7.26, 23.94; **bring up,** *allegare,* 3.15. For *allegare, see also* cite

brother, *fratello,* 8.36, 19.80; **Brother,** *fra',* 6.24

build, *edificare,* 6.25, 18.70, 20.83, 20.86, 20.87; **building,** *edificazione, edifizio,* 3.7, 6.25, 7.27, 25.98

burden (n.), *carico,* 22.93; **burden** (v.), *gravare,* 16.63 (2×), 19.78. For *carico, see also* blame; for *gravare, see also* grave

call, *chiamare,* 3.7, 3.16, 4.18, 7.26, 8.35, 8.36, 8.37, 9.39, 11.45, 13.54 (2×), 15.61, 17.68, 19.78, 19.82 (2×), 21.88

campaign (n.), *impresa,* 3.15, 7.28 (2×), 13.54, 16.63, 16.64, 21.88; **campaign** (n.), *compagna,* 14.59; **campaign** (v.), *campeggiare,*★ 12.53. For *impresa, see also* enterprise; undertaking; for *campagna, see also* country; field

capital, *capitale,* 14.60

captain (n.), *capitano,* 6.25, 8.35, 12.49 (3×), 12.50 (2×), 12.51 (3×), 12.52, 14.59, 19.78

capture, *espugnazione,* 7.28, 10.43, 19.81; **capture** (v.), *espugnare,* 12.51, 13.54

cardinal,★ *cardinale,* 3.16, 7.33, 11.47 (2×)

care, *cura,* ED.3 (2×), 14.59, 18.70; **care** (v.), *curare,* 11.45, 15.62, 16.63, 17.65, 17.67, 19.79. For *curare, see also* concern; cure

caress, *vezzeggiare,* 3.10

case,★ *caso,* 3.12, 6.24, 9.41, 9.42, 10.43(2×), 12.51, 16.64 (2×), 19.73, 21.89 (2×), 21.90, 23.95. *See also* chance

Castello, *Castello,* 20.86; **castle,** *castello,* 20.87

cause★ (n.), *cagione,* 2.7 (3×), 3.7, 3.8, 3.9 (2×), 3.10, 3.16, 4.18, 7.27, 7.33, 9.40, 11.45, 11.46 (2×), 12.48 (3×), 12.49, 13.56, 13.57, 14.58 (3×), 14.60, 17.67 (3×), 18.69 (2×), 19.75 (2×), 19.76 (2×), 19.77, 19.82, 20.85, 20.86 (2×), 24.96, 25.99; **cause** (n.), *causa,* 17.67; **cause** (v.), *causare,* 3.16 (3×), 9.39, 12.49

caution, *respetto,* 25.99, 25.100, 25.101; **cautious,** *respettivo,* 25.99 (2×), 25.100, 25.101 (2×). *See also* concern; hesitate; regard; respect

cavalry, *cavalleria,* 26.105 (2×). *Cf.* horse

centurion, *centurione,* 19.79, 19.80

century, *secolo,* 12.50

chance, *caso,* 14.60; **chance,** *sorte,* 12.51, 23.95, 25.98. For *caso, see also* case; for *sorte, see also* sort

change (n.), *variazione,* 18.70, 23.94, 26.105; **change** (n.), *mutazione,* 2.7, 22.93; **change** (n.), *alterazione,* 4.18, 11.47. For *variare, variazione, see also* variation

charity, *carità,* 18.70. *See also* love

chastity, *castità,* 14.60

check (v.), *frenare,* 7.31; **check** (v.), *tenere,*★ 12.50; **check** (v.), *raffrenare,* 19.72; **check** (n.), *freno,* 19.76. For *freno, see also* bit; *cf.* bridle

child, *figliuolo,* 17.66; *piccolo,* 8.35. For *figliuolo, see also* son

choose, *eleggere,* 23.94; **choice,** *elezione,* 7.33 (2×), 13.54, 22.92 (2×), 23.93. *See also* elect

Christian, *cristiano,* 19.82, 21.88

church,★ *chiesa,* 3.14 (3×), 3.15, 3.16, 7.27 (2×), 7.28, 7.31, 11.45, 11.46, 11.47 (4×), 12.51, 12.52 (2×), 21.88, 26.102

cite, cite before, *allegare, preallegare,* 3.15, 13.55, 17.65. *See also* bring up

citizen, *cittadino,* 5.20, 8.34 (2×), 8.35, 8.36 (2×), 8.37 (2×), 9.38, 9.39, 9.41, 9.42 (5×), 10.44, 12.49, 12.50 (2×), 12.52 (2×), 13.57, 17.67, 20.84, 21.91. *Cf.* city; civil

city,★ *città,* 5.20, 5.21, 7.30, 8.35 (2×), 8.36, 8.37 (2×), 9.39, 10.43, 10.44, 19.74, 21.91 (2×); *civitas* (L), 5.20 (T). *Cf.* citizen; civil

civil, *civile,* 7.30, 8.35, 8.37, 9.38, 9.39, 9.42, 21.89. *Cf.* citizen; city

civil life, *vita civile,* 21.89

colony, *colonia,* 3.10 (3×), 3.11 (2×), 3.12, 3.15

color, *colorire,* 18.69, 18.70. *See also* pretext

combat (n.), *combattere,* 26.104; **combat** (v.), *combattere,* 18.69, 19.72. *See also* battle; fight

command (v.), *comandare,* 7.26, 7.29, 9.39 (3×), 9.41, 9.42, 14.58, 18.71, 26.101, 26.104; **command** (n.), *comandamento,* 9.42; **command** (n.), *condotto,*★ 7.28. *Cf.* emperor; empire; imperial; king; reign; rule

common, *comune,* 10.44, 24.96, 24.97

community, *universalità*, 17.66; **community,** *università*, 19.76, 19.77, 21.91, 26.102. *See also* general; universal

company, being in, *fare compagnia*, 19.73, 21.90. *See also* associate

concern, * *cura*, 11.46 (2×), 19.75; **concern,** * *maneggio*, 19.72; **concern,** * *respetto*, 3.9. For *maneggio, respetto, see also* care; cure; regard; respect

condemn, *dannare*, 17.67

condottiere, *condottiere*,13.56

conduct (v.),* *governare*, 7.32, 9.40, 14.60. *See also* govern

confess, *confessare*, 12.51, 15.62

confidence, *confidenza*, 17.66; **have confidence,** *confidare*, ED.3, 26.104. *See also* trust; *cf.* belief

conform, *conformare*, 14.60, 25.99; **conformity,** *conformare*, 25.100. *Cf.* disparity; form; unlike

conjecture, *coniettura*, 22.92, 25.98

conquer, conquered, *vincere*, 4.17, 6.24, 7.32; **unconquerable,** *insuperabile*, 13.57. *See also* defeat; win; *cf.* victor, victory.

consent (v.), *consentire, acconsentire, consentimento*, 3.12, 3.15 (2×), 7.27, 7.33 (2×); **consent** (n.), *consenso*, 7.28. *See also* grant

conspire, *coniurare*, 19.72, 19.73 (4×), 19.74, 19.75; **conspire,** *conspirare, cospirare*, 8.37, 19.77, 19.80, 19.81; **conspiracy,** *coniura*, 19.72, 19.73 (2×), 19.74; **conspirator,** *coniuranti*, 19.73 (3×)

constitute, *costituire*, 19.75; **constitute,** *fare*, 23.93; **constitution,** *costituzione*, 6.24. For *costituzione, see also* institution; for *costituire, see also* establish

content, to become content, *contentare*, 4.18, 19.73, 20.86 (4×), 25.100; **content,** *contento*, 8.35, 19.72, 19.74 (2×); **malcontent,** *mal contento*, 3.11, 3.14, 4.18, 6.23, 8.37, 19.73 (2×). *See also* bad; evil

contract, *contratto*, 21.90

convenience, *posta*, "at his convenience" for *a sua posta*, 9.40, 17.68 (2×); **inconvenience,** *inconveniente*, 3.12, 21.91 (2×); *incomodità*, 11.46. For *incomodità, see also* advantage

corrupt, *corrompere*, 4.18 (2×), 19.77; **corrupting,** *corruzione*, 7.26; **corrupter,** *corruttore*, 17.68

council, *concilio*, 21.89; **council,** *consiglio*, 23.94. For *consiglio, see also* counsel

counsel (v.), *consigliare*, 23.95 (2×); **take counsel,** *consigliarsi*, 23.94, 23.95 (2×); **counsel** (n.), *consiglio*, 8.38, 9.40, 23.95(4×); **counselor,** *consigliere*,23.95. For *consiglio, see also* council

country, countryside, *paese,* 3.8, 10.43, 10.44, 14.59; *campagna,* 25.99; *provincia,* 26.104. For *campagna, see also* campaign; field; for *paese, see also* landscape; for *provincia, see also* province

course,* *partito,* 3.13 (2×), 3.14, 3.15, 13.54 (2×), 19.73, 19.76, 21.89, 21.91, 24.97. *See also* policy

court (n.), *iudicio, iudizio,* 7.30, 18.71. *See also* judge

covert, *copertamente,* 18.69

cowardice, cowardly, *viltà, vile,* 12.48, 20.83. *See also* base

create, recreate, *creare, recreare,* 5.20 (3×), 7.32 (2×), 7.33, 19.77 (2×); **creation,** *creazione,* 7.33

credit, *credito,* 4.18

criminal, *scellerato,* 8.34; **crime,** *scelleratezza,* 8.34, 8.35, 8.36, 8.37, 9.38; **of crime,** *scellerato,* 8.34; **crimes,** *scelera* (L), 8.34 (T)

cruel, cruelty, *crudele,* 7.29, 15.61, 17.65 (4×), 17.66, 17.67, 19.76, 19.80; **very cruel,** *crudelissimo,* 19.77, 19.81; **cruelty,*** *crudeltà,* 7.30, 8.35, 8.37 (3×), 10.44, 17.65, 17.67, 19.76 (3×), 19.79, 19.81 (2×), 21.88, 26.102; **cruelty,** *crudelitas* (L), 17.65 (T)

crush, *opprimere,* 20.85, 21.90. *See also* oppress

cunning, *arte,* 8.36. *See also* art

cure (v.), *curare,* 3.12 (2×); **cure** (v.), *guarire,* 26.102. For *curare, see also* care, concern

custom, *costume,* 3.9 (3×), 12.51; **custom,** *consuetudine,* 20.86; **customary,** *consueto, usarsi,** 8.36; *solere,* ED.3, ED.4; **customarily,** *solere,* 9.41, 17.66. For *consueto, solere, see also* accustom

danger, *pericolo, periculo, pericoloso, periculoso,* ED.4, 4.17, 6.23, 6.24, 7.27, 7.29, 8.35 (3×), 9.41, 9.42 (3×), 12.48, 12.53, 13.54, 13.55 (4×), 13.56, 16.63, 17.66 (2×), 19.72, 19.73, 19.78, 20.83, 21.90, 23.93

day,* *giornata,* 12.52. *See also* battle

death, *morte,* 7.31 (2×), 7.32 (2×), 9.42, 11.47, 12.50, 17.67, 19.73, 19.75, 19.78, 19.79; **death,** *mors* (L), 4.16 (T); **death,** *morire,* 19.77, 19.78 (2×), 19.79 (3×), 19.80 (2×). *See also* die; kill

debate (v.), *disputare,* 2.6. *See also* dispute

deceive, deceived, *ingannare, ingannarsi,* 3.8 (2×), 7.33, 8.37, 9.41 (2×), 18.70 (3×), 19.72, 19.78, 22.92, 23.93, 23.95; **deceit,** *inganno,* 7.29, 18.70

decent, *onesto,* 9.39, 19.77; **decency,** *onestà,* 9.39; **indecent,** *disoneste,* 21.90. *See also* honest; *cf.* honorable

decide, *deliberare,* 7.28, 8.34 (2×), 19.78, 23.94 (2×); **decide,** *volere,*

3.13, 7.27 (2×); **decision,** *deliberare, deliberazione,* 3.14, 19.78, 19.79, 20.83, 21.89, 23.94, 23.95

deed, *opera,* 6.24, 7.27, 14.59 (2×), 16.63, 19.77 (2×), 20.85, 22.92. *See also* work

defeat (v.), *rompere,* * 4.18, 8.35, 13.54, 20.84; **defeat** (v.), *vincere,* 4.18, 19.79, 21.89, 24.97; **defeated,** *battuto,* 3.11, 12.52. For *vincere, see also* conquer; overcome; win; *cf.* victor; victory

defend, *difendere, defendere,* 3.14, 6.24, 8.35, 8.37, 9.39, 9.41, 11.45, 11.47, 12.48, 12.50, 13.54 (2×), 13.57, 16.63, 16.64, 18.69 (2×), 18.71, 19.72, 19.73 (2×), 19.79, 20.84, 21.89, 23.93 (3×), 24.97, 26.104; **defend,** *difensione,* 10.42; **defense,** *difesa, difendere,* 8.35, 10.44 (3×), 11.46, 12.48, 14.59, 24.96, 24.97 (2×); **defender,** *defensore* 3.11, 6.23; **undefended,** *indifeso,* 11.45

demonstrate, *dimostrare,* 6.23, 12.49, 25.98

deserve, *meritare,* 3.15 (2×); **deserve,** *avere merito,* 20.83; **deserving,** *degno,* 6.22, 7.29, 19.80; **undeservedly,** *indegnamente,* ED.4; **undeserving,** *indegna,* ED.3. For *meritare, degno, see also* bought; merit; worthy; *cf.* indignation

desire (n.), *desiderio,* ED.4, 5.21, 25.100; **desire** (v.), *desiderare,* ED.3 (2×), 3.14, 4.18, 9.39 (2×), 15.61, 17.65, 22.93 (2×), 25.100

desperate, to make, *desperare,* 19.74. *Cf.* hope

die, *morire,* 4.17, 7.31 (3×), 7.32 (4×), 8.36, 9.42, 12.49, 12.50, 19.77, 20.87, 26.105; **die out,** *spegnere,* 26.103; **dead,** *morto,* 4.19, 8.35, 8.37, 19.74. *See also* kill; *cf.* homicide

dignity, *dignità,* 19.78, 19.80, 21.91; **dignity,** *dignitas* (L), 21.90. *Cf.* disdain; indignation; worthy

discipline, *disciplina,* 8.36, 12.48, 12.53, 14.58, 17.68, 18.69

discord, *discordare,* 25.99, 25.101

discourse (v.), *discorrere,* 11.45, 12.48 (2×), 12.52, 19.71; **discourse** (n.), *discorso,* 19.81, 19.82. For *discorrere, see also* discuss; review

discuss, *discorrere,* ED.4, 3.9, 4.19, 6.24, 7.27, 10.43, 11.46, 15.61, 19.75, 19.80, 20.86, 24.96, 25.99, 26.101; **discussion,** *ragionamento,* 8.36, 8.37, 25.100. For *discorrere, see also* discourse; review; *cf.* reason

disdain, *disprezzo,* 19.77, 19.82; **disdain,** *dedignazione,* 19.80. *Cf.* dignity; indignation; scorn; worthy

disparity, *disformità,* 3.9 (2×), 4.19; **disparate,** *disforme,* 3.9, 3.11, 3.13. *See also* unlike; *cf.* conform

dispute (v.), *disputare,* 15.61; **dispute** (n.), *disputa,* 17.66. For *disputare, see also* debate

dissension, *dissensione,* 17.67

dissimulate, *dissimulare,* 7.29; **dissimulator,** *dissimulatore,* 17.66, 18.70

dominion, *dominio,* 1.5, 1.6, 2.7 (2×), 24.97; **dominion,** *dominare,* 3.9; **dominion,** *dominazione,* 20.86; **domination,** *dominio,* 26.105. For *imperio, see also* empire; power; *cf.* imperial

doubtful, *dubbio, dubio,* 6.23, 13.55, 21.91; **without doubt,** *sanza, senza dubbio,* 20.85, 23.95. For *dubitare, see also* fear; hesitate; question

dread, *paura,* 17.67. *See also* afraid; fear

duke,* *duca,* 2.7, 3.9, 3.13, 7.26 (2×), 7.27 (3×), 7.28 (5×), 7.29 (4×), 7.30 (2×), 7.31, 7.32, 7.33 (2×), 11.46 (4×), 11.47, 12.50, 12.51, 13.55 (2×), 14.58 (2×), 20.86, 21.90, 24.96; **duchy,** *ducato,* 7.28, 7.29. *Cf.* lord; master

duty, *offizio,* 7.29, 8.36. *See also* office

effect, *effetto,* 9.39, 17.67, 23.94, 25.99

effeminate, *effeminato,* 6.23, 15.62, 19.72, 19.77, 20.84

efficacy, *efficacia,* 18.70

elect, *eleggere,* 19.80; **elected,** *eletto,* 19.78 (2×), 19.82. For *eleggere, see also* choose

eliminate, *spegnere,* 2.7, 3.9 (3×), 3.10, 3.15, 4.18 (3×), 4.19 (2×), 5.21 (2×), 6.23, 6.24, 6.25, 7.26, 7.28 (2×), 7.29, 7.30, 7.31, 7.32 (2×), 8.38, 11.46 (2×), 11.47 (3×), 13.55, 13.56 (2×), 16.63, 18.69, 19.81, 25.98. *See also* die

emperor, *imperadore, imperatore,* 7.26, 10.43, 12.52, 13.54, 19.75 (3×), 19.76 (3×), 19.77, 19.78 (4×), 19.82, 23.94 (2×). *Cf.* command; empire; imperial; king; reign; rule

empire, *imperio,* 1.5, 4.19, 6.23, 7.26, 7.31, 7.32, 8.35, 12.50, 12.52, 13.57 (2×), 16.64 (2×), 17.68, 19.75 (2×), 19.77 (2×), 19.78 (2×), 19.80 (2×), 19.81 (2×). *See also* power; *cf.* command; emperor; imperial; king; reign; rule

employ,* *operare,* 12.49. See also work

enslaved, *stiavo,* 6.23, 12.53, 26.102 (2×). *Cf.* servant

enterprise, *impresa,* 3.15, 4.18, 11.47, 12.51, 21.87, 21.88, 25.100 (2×), 26.105; **undertake enterprises,** *fare imprese,* 20.85, 21.88. *See also* campaign; undertaking

envy, *invidia,* 3.11, 6.25, 7.31, 26.105

equal, equally, *equale, equalmente,* 9.39, 25.99; **equal,** *retto,* 7.32. For *equalmente, see also* identically

err, *errare,* 3.10, 7.33, 17.68

error, *errore,* 3.13, 3.14, 3.15 (3×), 7.30, 12.51, 13.56, 17.68, 22.92, 23.93

establish,* *osservare,* 3.10; **establish,** *costituire,* 8.34. For *osservare, see also* observe; for *costituire, see also* constitute

evil, *male,* 3.12, 3.13 (2×), 8.37, 8.38, 9.40, 10.44 (2×), 13.57, 14.58, 18.70, 19.73, 22.92. *See also* bad; ill; irresolute; malcontent; *cf.* malignity

exalt, *esaltare,* 11.45. *See also* extol

examine, *esaminare,* ED.3, 3.13, 6.23, 6.24, 9.40, 10.42, 14.60, 19.79

example, *esemplo,* 3.12, 4.17, 6.22, 6.25 (2×), 7.26, 7.27, 7.33, 8.34, 12.52, 13.54, 13.55, 13.57, 17.65, 18.69, 18.70, 19.74, 19.75, 20.84, 20.86, 21.87, 21.88 (2×), 21.90, 21.91, 23.94, 24.96, 26.103; **example,** *exemplum* (L), 2.7, 5.20, 12.50; **example,** *esempio,* 13.54; **for example,** *verbigrazia,* 14.59

excellent,* *eccellente,* 6.22, 6.23, 7.30, 8.36, 12.49, 14.60 (2×), 19.72, 21.89, 21.91, 22.92, 26.104; **most excellent,** *eccellentissimo,* 6.22, 7.30, 8.35 (2×), 19.79, 22.92

excess, *eccesso,* 19.73; **excessive,*** *eccessivo,* 2.7, 7.30

excuse (n.), *scusa,* 3.15, 25.101; **excuse** (v.), *scusare,* 20.83; *escurare,* 3.15, 17.68

execution, *esecuzione,* 17.66, 19.73

expectation, *opinione,* 13.54. *See also* opinion

experience, *esperienza,* ED.3, 3.8, 3.16, 6.24, 12.50, 18.69, 19.73, 26.104; **experience,** *practica,* 14.59. For *esperienza, see also* experiment; test

experiment, *esperienza,* 26.105. *See also* experience; test

external, *esterno,* 7.29, 8.37, 19.72, 20.84. *See also* foreign; outside

extol, *esaltare,* 22.92. *See also* exalt

extraordinary, *estraordinario,* 2.7 (2×), 7.27, 16.63, 19.76, 21.88, 21.89, 26.103; **extraordinarily,** *estraordiamente,* 16.63, 19.81. *Cf.* ordinary; order

faction, *fazione,* 11.46 (2×), 11.47

failure, *infelicità,* 12.49. *See also* happy

faith, *fede,* 3.15 (2×), 8.35, 12.48, 12.51, 17.65, 18.68, 18.69 (2×), 18.70 (2×), 18.71, 19.73, 20.83, 20.85, 26.105; *fides* (L), 18.68 (T); **faithful,** *fedele,* 3.10, 7.26, 7.28, 9.42, 15.62, 18.70, 20.83 (2×); *in fede,* 17.65; *fide,* 26.104; *fidele,* 22.92 (2×); **faithfully,** *con fede,* 20.85; **infidel,** *infidele,* 13.55; **infidelity,** *infidelità,* 18.70; **unfaithful,** *infedele,* 7.32, 12.48, 13.55; **breaker of faith,** *fedifrago,* 15.62. *Cf.* trust; believe

fame, *fama,* 17.68, 21.88, 21.89; *fama* (L), 13.57. *Cf.* infamy
father, *padre,* 7.27, 7.32, 12.50, 13.56, 13.57, 17.67, 19.74, 19.80,
    24.97; **fatherless,** *sanza padre,* 8.35; **Father,** *Pre',* 23.94; **grand-**
    father, *avolo,* 19.74. *Cf.* maternal; mother; parricide; patrimony
fatherland, *patria,* 6.23 (2✕), 8.34, 8.36, 8.37, 9.38, 9.41, 26.105
fault, *colpa,* 7.27
favor (n.), *grazia,* ED.3, 4.17 (2✕), 7.26, 7.33, 19.75; **favor** (v.),
    favorire, 12.51, 19.75 (3✕); **unfavorable,** *non buono,* 22.92.
    For *grazia, see also* grace; for *favorire, favore, see also* support
fear (v.), *temere,* 3.10, 3.11, 4.18 (2✕), 7.27, 7.32, 7.33, 9.39, 9.40
    (2✕), 10.43, 12.51 (2✕), 12.52, 17.66 (3✕), 17.67 (2✕), 17.68
    (2✕), 19.73 (3✕), 19.74, 19.79 (3✕), 19.81, 21.89, 21.91, 22.93;
    fear (v.), *dubitare,* 4.18, 7.30, 7.31, 15.61; **fear** (n.), *paura,* 3.11,
    6.23, 7.31, 7.33, 8.37, 12.53, 19.72, 19.73, 19.75, 19.81, 20.86
    (2✕), 21.91, 25.100, 25.101; **fear** (n.), *sospetto,* 21.88; **fear** (n.),
    timore, 3.10, 10.44, 12.48, 17.67, 19.78, 21.91; **feared,** *timeo* (L),
    17.65 (T); **fearful,** *pauroso,* 3.14; **fearsome,** *pauroso,* 8.37; **make**
    oneself feared, *si fare paura,* 17.66; For *paura, see also* afraid;
    dread; for *dubitare, see also* hesitate; question
ferocious, *feroce,* 25.101; **fierce,** *feroce,* 15.62, 19.79; **ferocity,** *ferocità,*
    7.30; **ferocity,** *ferocia,* 7.31, 19.79, 19.81, 25.100
fever, *febbre,* 13.57
few,* *pochi,* 4.17, 7.28, 8.38, 9.39, 9.41, 9.42, 12.53, 13.57, 16.63
    (2✕), 18.71 (4✕), 19.72, 19.73, 26.104; **very few,** *pochissimi,*
    7.31, 9.39, 17.65. *See also* little; oligarchical
field, *campagna,* 4.18, 4.19, 10.43, 24.97. *See also* campaign; country
fight (v.), *combattere,* 4.19, 12.51, 13.56, 19.80, 21.90; **fight** (v.), *fare una*
    giornata, 10.43; **fight** (v.), *militare,* 8.36, 13.56, 17.67; **fighting,**
    militava, 8.34. For *combattere, see also* battle; combat; for *militare,*
    see also soldier
fitting, *conveniente,* 15.61, 19.82. *See also* convenience; suitable
force (v.), *forzare,* 3.13, 6.23, 6.24 (2✕), 8.38, 11.47, 16.64, 19.76,
    19.77, 20.85; **force** (n.), *forza,* 2.7, 3.8, 3.11 (2✕), 3.15, 3.16,
    4.18, 7.26, 7.29, 7.31 (2✕), 11.46 (2✕), 13.57, 18.69, 20.84,
    26.104; **force,** *vis* (L), 10.42 (T), 13.57; **by force,** *per forza,* 6.24,
    7.32. *Cf.* strength
foreign, *esterno,* 12.50; **foreign,** *forestiero,* 3.12; **foreigner,** *esterno,*
    26.104; **foreign,** *forestiero,* 3.11 (2✕), 3.15, 11.46, 12.49, 12.52,
    13.54, 20.86, 20.87 (4✕). For *esterno, see also* external; outside
form (n.), *forma,* 6.23, 26.102, 26.104. *Cf.* conform

former,* *antiquo,* 4.19, 7.28. *See also* ancient; antiquity; old

fortify, *fortificare,* 10.43 (3×). *Cf.* fortress; strength

fortress,* *fortezza,* 20.83, 20.84, 20.86 (5×), 20.87 (6×); **fortress,** *arces* (L), 20.83 (T). *See also* strength; *cf.* fortify

fortune, *fortuna,* ED.4 (2×), 1.6, 3.9, 6.22 (3×), 6.23, 6.25 (2×), 7.25, 7.26 (4×), 7.27 (3×), 7.28, 7.31, 7.32, 8.34 (2×), 8.35 (2×), 9.39, 9.40, 11.45, 11.46, 12.51, 13.54, 13.56, 13.57, 14.58, 14.60, 17.67, 18.70, 20.85, 21.89, 21.90, 24.97, 25.98 (3×), 25.99 (2×), 25.100, 25.101 (2×), 26.102 (2×), 26.104; **fortune,** *fortuna* (L), 7.25 (T), 25.98 (T); **fortunate,** *fortunata,* 9.39

found (v.), *fondare,* 6.22, 6.23, 8.38, 9.41 (3×), 9.42, 12.48, 17.66, 17.68, 18.69, 19.75, 19.82, 23.95, 26.104; **founder,** *fondatore,* 6.23

foundation, *fondamento,* 6.25, 7.26, 7.27, 7.29, 7.32 (2×), 9.41 (2×), 12.48 (2×), 21.88 (2×), 26.104; **great foundation,** *granfondamento,* 7.27; **to the foundation,** *funditus* (L), 20.86

fraud, *fraude,* 7.32

free (adj.), *libero,* 1.6, 3.9, 5.20 (2×), 5.21 (2×), 12.50; **very free,** *liberissimo,* 10.43, 12.50; **freely,** *liberamente,* 23.94; **free** (v.), *liberare,* 8.35; *liberta* (L), 26.101 (T); **free will,** *libero arbitrio,* 25.98, 26.103; **freedom,** *libero arbitrio,* 23.94. *Cf.* liberal; liberate; liberty; will

frighten, *sbigottire,* 9.41, 11.47, 18.69. *See also* terrible

future, *futuro,* 3.8, 3.12, 7.27 (2×), 7.31, 8.36

gain,* *guadagnare,* 3.11, 3.13, 5.21, 7.28, 7.29, 7.30, 7.32, 8.35, 8.38, 9.40 (2×), 11.47, 20.83, 20.86; **regain,** *riguadagnare,* 3.13. *See also* win; *cf.* acquire

general, *generale,* 3.16, 23.95; **in general,** *in universale,* 18.71, 25.99; **generally,** *generalmente,* 12.48, 17.66; **generality,** *generalità,* 19.71; *universalità,* 19.72; **the people generally,** *università, universale,* 19.73, 19.76; **generality of people,** *universale,* 9.41, 19.75. *See also* community; universal

generate, *generare,* 7.30; **generate,** *concepere,* 20.84; **regeneration,** *generazione,* 26.105. *See also* kind

gentleman, gentry, *gentile uomo,* 7.28 (2×), 7.31 (2×), 12.51

glory, *gloria,* 7.26, 8.35, 14.60, 17.68 (2×), 21.88, 24.96, 25.99, 26.103; **glorify,** *gloriare,* 14.60; **glorious,** *glorioso,* 19.82; **gloriously,** *gloriosamente,* 12.51

God, god, *Dio,* 6.22 (2×), 8.38, 11.45, 12.48, 25.98, 26.102 (3×), 26.103 (3×)

gold, *oro,* ED.3

goodness, *bontà,* 11.47, 19.77

govern, *governare,* 2.6, 4.17 (4×), 4.18, 11.45, 12.52, 12.53, 19.74 (2×), 19.77, 21.88, 23.95, 25.98 (3×), 25.100; **ungoverned,** *non governato,* 11.45; **for governing,** *al governo,* 19.74; **governing** (n.), *governi,* 10.43; **government,** *governo,* ED.4, 4.17, 4.19, 7.28, 7.29, 8.37, 12.52, 15.61, 17.67, 17.68, 19.74, 19.81 (2×), 25.100; **governor,** *governatore,* 23.95. For *governare, see also* conduct; for *governo, see also* arrangements

grace, *grazia,* 6.22. *See also* favor; grateful

grant, *consentire,* 7.28. *See also* consent

grateful, *conoscente,* 19.79; *grado,* 8.38; **ungrateful,** *ingrato,* 17.66; **ingratitude,** *ingratitudine,* 19.79, 21.90. For *grado, see also* rank

grave, *grave,* 8.36, 15.62, 19.79; **grave one,** *gravo,* 3.10; **gravity,** *gravità,* ED.4, 19.72. *See also* burden; slow

happy, *felice,* 6.23 (2×), 6.25, 11.45, 19.82, 25.99, 25.100, 25.101; **happy,** *felicitando,* 25.100; **happily,** *felicemente,* 19.78; **unhappy,** *infelice,* 19.82, 25.99, 25.101; **unhappiness,** *infelicità,* 14.58; **be happy** (v.), *felicitare,* 25.99 (2×). For *infelicità, see also* failure

hate, *odiare,* 10.43, 17.67, 19.73 (2×), 19.76 (2×), 19.77, 19.79, 19.80, 20.87 (3×); **hate,** *avere in odio,* 20.87; **make hated,** *fare odiare,* 2.7, 10.44, 19.75; **hate,** *fare odioso,* 16.63, 19.72, 19.80; **hated,** *odioso,* 16.65; **hatred,** *odio,* 5.21, 7.30, 7.33, 16.65 (2×), 17.67, 17.68, 19.74, 19.75, 19.76, 19.77 (3×), 19.79, 19.81, 19.82, 20.83, 20.87; **hatred,** *odio* (L.), 19.71 (T); **hateful,** *odioso,* 7.30, 16.65, 19.72; **most hateful,** *odiosissimo,* 19.79

head, *capo*,* 3.11, 4.18, 6.23, 7.28, 7.29, 11.47, 12.50, 13.55, 13.56, 19.78, 26.102, 26.103, 26.104 (2×)

heart, *core,* 9.41; **heart,** *cor,* 26.105

heir, *erede,* 11.47, 19.82. *Cf.* hereditary

hereditary, *ereditario, hereditario,* 1.5 (2×), 2.6, 19.77, 19.80, 19.82 (3×), 20.85, 24.96; **hereditary,** *hereditariis* (L), 2.6 (T). *See also* heir; *cf.* right, hereditary

hesitate, *dubitare,* 10.44, 13.55; **hesitation,** *rispetto, respetto,* 3.10, 10.43, 15.62, 17.66, 21.89, 23.95; **hesitant,** *respettivo,* 3.8; **hesitant,** *con respetto,* 7.33. For *dubitare, see also* doubtful; fear; question; for *rispetto, respetto, see also* concern; regard; respect

history, *istoria,* 13.54, 14.60, 20.84

Holiness, *Santità,* 11.47

homage, *servitù,* ED.3; **homage,** *ossequio,* 26.105. *Cf.* servant

homicide, *omicidio,* 8.37, 19.74. *Cf.* die; kill
honest, *intero,* 15.62, 18.70; **total,** *intero,* 13.55; **honesty,** *integrità,* 18.70; **honestly,** *con integrità,* 18.68
honor (n.), *onore,* 8.36 (2×), 9.40, 19.72, 22.93 (3×), 26.102, 26.103; **honorable,** *onorevole,* 8.36, 18.71; **honor** (v.), *onorare,* ED.4, 6.25, 7.28, 9.40, 12.53, 21.88, 21.91, 22.93, 26.101, 26.104; **honorably,** *onoratamente,* 8.36 (2×); **most honorably,** *onoratissimo,* 19.77
hope (v.), **to put hope in,** *sperare,* 4.18 (4×), 9.40, 11.47, 19.73 (2×), 22.92, 24.97, 26.102, 26.103; **hope** (n.), *speranza,* 10.44, 26.105; *spes* (L), 26.103. *Cf.* desperate
horse, *cavallo,* ED.3, 7.29, 12.53, 19.81, 26.104, 26.105; **horseman,** *cavallo,* 8.36; **on horse,** *a cavallo,* 8.37. *Cf.* cavalry
human, *umano,* 11.45, 15.62, 25.98, 25.100; **human,** *humanus* (L), 25.98 (T); **inhuman,** *inumano,* 17.67. *See also* humane
humane, *umano,* 15.62, 18.70, 19.76; **humanity,** *umanità,* ED.3, 14.60, 17.66, 18.70 (2×), 21.91; **inhumanity,** *inumanità,* 8.35. *See also* human
humor, *umore,* 9.39, 19.76, 19.77
hurt,★ *offendere,* 3.15, 8.37, 13.55, 16.63, 17.66 (2×), 19.79, 20.86; **unhurt,** *inoffeso,* 3.10. *See also* attack; offend
identically, *equalmente,* 25.99. *See also* equal
idle, idly, *ozioso,* 10.44, 14.60. *See also* leisure
illness, *male,* 3.12; **ill,** *male,* 6.24, 12.48, 21.89
imagine, *imaginare,* 15.61 (2×); **imagination,** *imaginazione,* 15.61
imitate, *imitare,* 6.22 (2×), 7.29, 8.34, 14.60 (3×), 19.78, 19.82 (3×); **imitation,** *imitazione,* 6.22, 14.60; **to be imitated,** *imitabile,* 7.32
imperial, *imperiale,* 19.80 (2×). *Cf.* command; emperor; empire; imperial; king; reign; rule
impetuosity, *impeto,* 25.99, 25.100 (2×); **impetuous,**★ *impetuoso,* 25.99, 25.100, 25.101; **impetuously,** *impetuosamente,* 25.100; **impetus,** *impeto,* 25.98 (3×). *See also* thrust, uprising
indignation, *sdegno,* 19.81. *See also* disdain; scorn; *cf.* dignity; worthy
industry, *industria,* 2.6, 3.9, 3.12, 3.16, 10.43, 12.53 (2×), 14.60, 19.76
infamy, *infamia,* 14.58, 15.62 (2×), 16.63 (2×), 16.65 (2×), 17.65, 19.72. *Cf.* fame
infantry, *fanteria,* 12.53, 13.56 (2×), 26.104, 26.105 (3×); **infantry,** *fanto,* 3.10, 12.53 (2×), 13.56, 19.81, 26.104, 26.105

infinite, *infinito,* 3.8, 3.11, 4.18, 7.29, 8.35, 8.37, 11.47, 16.63, 17.67
　　(2×), 18.69, 19.73, 19.74 (2×), 19.79

injure, *iniuriare,* 19.76, 25.100; **injury,** *iniuria,* 3.8, 7.33, 8.38 (2×),
　　9.39, 19.78, 19.79

innovate, *innovare,* 4.18, 21.88; **innovation,** *innovazione,* 2.7; **innovator,** *innovatore,* 6.24. *See also* new; *cf.* renew

insolent, *insolente,* 19.76; **insolence,** *insolenzia,* 7.29, 17.68, 19.75,
　　19.76, 24.97

inspire, *animare,* 9.4, 21.91. *See also* spirit

instability, *variazioni,* 3.7; **unstable,** *instabile,* 7.26; **unstable,** *instabile*
　　(L), 13.57. For *variazione, see also* change; variation

institution, *costituzione,* 19.74; **institution,** *ordine,* 10.44

insult, *insolenzia,* 26.102. *See also* insolence; *cf.* blame

intent, *animo,* 7.29, 7.30, 19.73; **intent,** *intento,* 11.46, 15.61;
　　intention, *intenzione,* 7.32, 12.49. *See also* mind; spirit; *cf.* magnanimous; pusillanimous

internal, *intrinseca,* 20.86

irresolute, *mal resoluto,* 21.90. For *male, see also* evil

judge (v.), *giudicare,* ED.3; **judge** (v.), *iudicare,* 7.27, 7.29, 7.30, 7.32,
　　8.34, 8.35, 8.38, 10.43 (2×), 12.52, 13.55 (2×), 18.71 (2×),
　　19.75, 19.77, 19.78, 20.83, 20.85, 20.86, 22.92, 25.98 (2×),
　　25.100, 25.101, 26.102; **without a trial,** *iniudicato,* 19.77; **judge**
　　(n.), *iudice,* 19.75; **judgment,** *iudicio,* 22.92; *iudizio,* 22.92; *sentenzia,* 13.57, 19.72, 20.83. For *iudizio, iudicio, see also* court; *cf.* just

just, *iusto,* 26.103, 26.105; *iustus* (L), 26.103; **justice,** *giustizia,* 21.90;
　　justice, *iustizia,* 19.76, 26.103; **justification,** *iustificazione,*
　　17.67. For *iusto, see also* adequate; *cf.* judge

kill, *ammazzare,* 7.31, 8.35, 8.37, 12.52, 12.53, 19.74 (2×), 19.77,
　　19.79 (2×), 19.81; **be killed,** *morire,* 19.75; **be killed,** *uccidere,*
　　8.34; **killing** (n.), *occisione,* 17.65, 19.79. For *morire, see also* die;
　　cf. homicide

kind★ (n.), *generazione,* 17.67, 18.69, 22.92; **kind**★ (n.), *genera* (L), 1.5
　　(T), 12.48 (T); **kind**★ (n.), *qualità,* 11.45, 16.63, 19.78; *ragione,*
　　7.29 (2×); **diverse kinds,** *diversità,* 4.17. For *generazione, see also*
　　generate; for *qualità, see also* quality; for *ragione, see also* reason

king, *re,* 1.6, 3.13 (2×), 3.14 (4×), 3.15, 4.17 (3×), 6.23, 7.28 (3×),
　　7.30 (2×), 7.33, 8.34, 11.45 (2×), 11.46, 12.49, 12.50, 13.54,
　　16.63, 16.64, 19.74, 19.75 (3×), 21.88 (3×), 24.96, 25.100 (3×),
　　25.101; **of being a king,** *regnandum* (L.), 6.25; **King,** *re,* 3.13
　　(2×), 3.15, 3.16, 7.28, 13.56 (2×); **kingdom,** *regno,* 1.6, 3.12,

3.14 (2×), 3.15, 4.17 (2×), 4.18 (4×), 4.19 (2×), 6.22, 7.30,
7.31, 7.33, 12.50, 12.51, 13.56 (2×), 13.57, 19.74 (2×), 19.75,
19.81, 19.82, 21.88, 24.97, 25.100; **kingdom,** *regnum* (L.), 4.16
(T), 6.25, 17.66; **kingdom,** *Reame,* 26.102; **kingly,** *regio,* 7.29.
Cf. queen

knowledge, ★ *cognizione,* ED.3, 14.59 (4×)

land, *terra,* 3.14, 17.67; **on land,** *in terra,* 12.51 (3×). *See also* town

landscape, *paese,* ED.4. *See also* country; *cf.* land

language, *lingua,* 3.9 (3×), 15.61

lasciviousness, *lascivo,* 15.62

law, *legge,* 3.9, 5.20 (3×), 6.23, 12.48 (4×), 12.50, 18.69, 19.73, 24.96,
26.104; *legibus* (L), 5.20 (T)

lead, ★ *governare,* 3.12, 7.32, 9.40, 12.53, 14.60, 17.67. *See also* conduct;
govern

legate, *legato,* 17.68 (2×), 21.89 (2×)

leisure, *ozioso,* 4.19, 21.88. *See also* idle

liberal, *liberale,* 7.32, 15.61, 16.62, 16.63, 16.64 (3×); **very liberal,** *liberalissimo,* 16.64; **liberality,** *liberalità,* 14.60, 16.62, 16.63 (2×),
16.64 (5×), 16.65; **liberality,** *del liberale,* 16.63 (4×), 16.65;
liberality, *liberalitate* (L.), 16.62 (T). *Cf.* free; liberty; liberate;
will

liberate, *liberare,* 9.41, 13.56. *Cf.* free; liberal; liberty; will

liberty, *libertà,* 5.20, 5.21 (2×), 8.36, 9.39, 12.50, 19.74. *Cf.* free;
liberal; liberate; will

license, *licenzia,* 9.39, 17.68; **in license,** *licenziosamente,* 19.77; **licentious,** *licenzioso,* 19.80. *See also* wanton

life, *vita,* 5.21, 6.23, 7.32, 8.34, 10.43, 11.46, 14.60 (2×), 17.66, 19.75,
19.76, 19.77, 19.79, 25.101, 26.103; *sangue,* 17.67 (2×). For
sangue, see also blood

little, *pochi,* 8.35. *See also* few; oligarchical

live freely, *vivere libero,* 3.9, 5.20, 5.21 (2×)

lord, *signore,* 1.5, 3.8 (2×), 3.13, 3.14 (2×), 3.15, 4.17 (5×), 4.18,
4.19, 7.27, 7.29, 7.31 (3×), 11.45, 18.69, 19.81, 19.82 (2×),
22.92, 24.96; **become lord,** *insignorirsi,* 7.27, 19.78. *See also*
Signor; *cf.* master

love (n.), *amore,* 4.17, 12.48, 17.66, 17.67, 21.90, 26.105; **love** (n.),
carità, 10.44; **love** (v.), *amare,* 2.7, 3.10, 4.17, 7.32, 9.40, 17.66
(3×), 17.68 (2×), 19.76 (3×), 19.79; **love,** *amari* (L), 17.65 (T);
lover, *amatore,* 19.76, 21.91. For *carità, see also* charity

Madonna, madonna, 3.13. *Cf.* woman

magistracy, magistrate, *magistrato,* 8.37, 9.41, 9.42 (3×)

magnanimous, *magnanimo,* 7.32. *Cf.* intent; pusillanimous; spirit

magnificent, *magnifico,* ED.3 (T), ED.3 (2×), ED.4 (3×)

majesty, *maestà,* 18.71, 19.73, 19.80, 21.91, 23.94

malcontent, *mal contento,* 3.11, 19.73 (2×). For *contento, see also* content; for *male, see also* evil

malignity, *malignità,* ED.4, 7.27. *Cf.* bad; evil

man, *uomo, passim.;* **men,** *gente,* 7.28, 8.35, 13.54; **men-at-arms,** *gente d'arme,* 3.8, 3.10, 3.11, 13.56 (2×); **men, wise,** *savi,* 3.13. For *gente, see also* troops

manage, *maneggiare,* 3.13, 6.23, 9.39, 10.43, 13.55, 16.64, 20.85

manoeuvers, *maneggi,* 26.103

marriage, *matrimonio,* 3.15, 7.28

marvel (v.) *maravigliare,* 4.16, 4.19, 6.21, 19.79; **marvel** (n.), *maraviglia,* 26.103; **marvelous,** *maraviglioso,* 19.79, 26.103

master (n.), *maestro,* 8.37. *Cf.* Signor; lord

maternal, *materno,* 8.35. *Cf.* mother; father

matter, *materia,* ED.4, 3.16, 6.23, 7.29, 15.61, 19.73, 19.74 (2×), 19.82, 20.83, 20.85, 21.89, 26.102, 26.104

medicine, *medicina,* 3.8, 3.12

memory, *memoria,* 2.7, 4.17, 4.19 (2×), 5.21, 7.26, 11.45, 13.56, 17.68, 19.74

mercenary, *mercenario,* 12.48 (3×), 12.49 (3×), 12.50 (3×), 12.52, 13.54, 13.55 (4×), 13.56, (3×), 13.57, 20.84; **mercenary,** *mercenariis* (L), 12.48 (T)

mercy,★ *pietà,* 8.35, 17.65 (2×), 17.68, 18.70; **mercy,** *pietate,* 17.65; **merciful,** *pietoso,* 15.62, 17.65 (3×), 18.70. For *pietà, see also* piety

merit, *merito* (n.) 3.12, 8.34. *Cf.* deserve; worthy

military, *militare,* 8.37, 10.44, 12.53, 17.68, 19.76, 19.79, 24.97, 26.103; **military,** *milizia,* 6.25, 7.32, 8.34, 8.35, 8.36 (2×), 12.52, 13.56, 14.58, 17.68, 20.84, 21.88; **military,** *militae,* 12.48; **military,** *militibus* (L), 12.52; **military,** *militiam* (L), 14.58 (T). For *militare, see also* fight; soldier; for *militibus* (L), *see also* soldier

mind, *animo,* 7.28 (2×), 21.88 (2×); **mind,** *mente,* 11.45, 14.59, 14.60. For *animo, see also* spirit; intent; *cf.* magnanimous; pusillanimous

minister, *ministro* (n.), 4.17 (2×), 7.30, 22.92 (5×), 22.93 (6×). *Cf.* administer

miracle, *miracolo,* 3.16; **miraculous,** *miracoloso,* 12.52

mixed, *misto,* 3.7, 12.48 (2×), 13.56, 17.67; **mixed,** *mixtus* (L), 13.54 (T); **mixed,** *mixtis* (L), 3.7 (T)

mode, *modo, passim;* **his own mode,** *a suo modo,* 23.94 (2×), 25.101. *See also* suitable

modern, *moderno,* ED.3, 8.34, 18.69, 20.86. 23.94

monarchy, *monarchia,* 4.17. *Cf.* king; queen

mother, *madre,* 19.77. *Cf.* father; maternal

multitude, *moltitudine,* 4.17, 6.24, 17.67

name (v.), *nominare,* 13.55, 13.57, 18.71, 26.103; **name** (v.), *prenominare,*12.48, 19.82, 26.103; **name** (n.), *nome,* 5.21 (2×), 16.63 (4×), 16.64, 16.65 (3×), 17.65, 17.66, 17.67 (2×)

nature,* *natura,* ED.4 (2×), 4.18, 6.24, 7.26, 7.30, 10.44, 14.59 (2×), 17.68 (2×), 18.69, 18.70, 19.76, 19.78, 23.95, 25.99, 25.100 (3×); **natural,** *naturale,* 2.7, 3.7, 3.8, 3.14, 4.17, 9.40, 20.86; **naturally,** *naturalmente,* 2.7

necessary, *necessario,* 3.10, 3.15, 4.18, 4.19, 6.23, 6.24, 7.27, 7.29, 7.30, 7.32, 8.36, 8.38, 9.39, 9.41, 12.48, 14.59, 15.61, 15.62, 16.63, 16.64 (2×), 17.67, 18.69, 18.70 (4×), 19.73, 19.75, 19.76, 19.78, 19.81 (3×), 19.82 (2×), 20.83, 20.84 (3×), 20.85, 25.101, 26.102 (2×), 26.104 (2×); **necessary,** *necessarium* (L), 26.103; **be necessary,** *necessitare,* 3.14, 7.31, 8.34, 8.35, 8.38, 9.40, 10.43, 12.52, 16.63, 16.65, 18.69, 18.70 (2×), 19.79; **necessity,** *necessità,* 2.7, 3.7, 3.15, 8.35, 8.38 (2×), 10.42, 10.43, 12.48, 13.56, 15.61, 18.70, 20.85, 21.90, 22.92, 23.95

nephew, *nipote,* 8.36

neutral, *neutrale,* 21.89 (2×), 21.90

neutrality, *neutralità,* 21.90

new, *nuovo, passim. Cf.* innovate

noble, *nobile,* 12.52; **ennobled,** *nobilitato,* 6.23, 26.105; **nobility,** *nobilità,* 17.66

oath, *giuramento,* 18.70

obey, *obedire,* 4.17, 5.21, 8.37, 9.39, 9.42 (2×), 10.43, 12.51, 14.58, 18.70, 26.104; **bring to obey,** *viene alla obedienza,* 12.50; **resolved to obey,** *alla obedienzia,* 13.55; **obedience,** *obedienza,* 7.29, 26.105

oblige, obligate, *obligare,*13.56, 22.93, 24.96; **obligation,** *obligo,*

7.33, 8.34, 10.44, 17.66, 20.83, 21.90; **obligated,** *obligato,* 3.8,
4.18, 20.83; **be obligated,** *obligarsi,* 9.40 (5×), 10.44; **obliged,**
obligato, 13.57; **release** (v.), *disobligare,* 11.46. *See also* pledge

observe, *osservare,* 3.11, 3.14, 3.16 (3×), 6.24, 8.38, 14.60, 15.62,
18.69 (3×), 18.70 (3×), 18.71, 19.73, 24.96 (2×); **observance,**
osservanzia, 18.69. For *osservare, see also* establish

obstinate, *ostinato,* 19.73, 19.79, 23.94, 25.101, 26.104, 26.105

offend, *offendere,* 2.7, 3.8 (2×), 3.10 (4×), 3.11, 7.32, 7.33 (4×), 8.38,
13.55, 16.63, 17.66, 19.73, 20.83, 23.94; **offense,** *offesa,* 3.10
(2×), 8.38, 12.48. *See also* attack, hurt

office, *offizio,* 11.45, 12.49; **official** (n.), *officiale,* 3.10; **official** (n.),
offiziale, 4.17. For *offizio, see also* duty

old, *vecchio,* 3.9, 5.21, 6.23, 6.25, 7.33, 12.48, 13.56, 19.77, 19.82
(2×), 20.84; **old,** *antiquo,* 7.32; **old,** *antico,* 6.25; **grown old,**
antiquato, 11.45, 24.96. For *antiquo, antico, see also* ancient

oligarchical, *di pochi,* 5.20 (2×). For *pochi, see also* few; little

opinion, *opinione,* 3.8, 9.41, 13.57, 14.60, 18.71, 19.72 (2×), 19.75,
19.80, 20.83, 20.85, 23.94, 23.95, 25.98 (3×). *See also* expectation; *cf.* believe; reputation; trust

opportunity, *occasione,* 3.8, 4.18, 6.23 (5×), 6.24, 6.25, 7.28, 7.30,
7.31, 9.39, 11.47, 13.55, 17.67, 20.84, 20.85, 21.89, 26.102,
26.103, 26.105

oppress, *opprimere,* 4.18, 6.23, 6.25, 9.39 (4×), 9.40, 9.41, 12.49 (2×),
12.50 (2×), 12.52, 26.102; **oppressed,** *oppressato,* 26.102. *See
also* crush

order (n.), *ordine, passim;* **order** (v.), *ordinare, passim;* **disorder,**★ *dis-
ordine,* 3.10, 3.15, 4.18, 17.65, 20.87; **disorder,**★ *discordia,* 11.47;
disorder (v.), *disordinare,* 7.27. For *ordine, see also* institution

ordinance, *ordinanza,* 13.56

ordinary, *ordinario,* 2.6, 3.8, 3.14, 3.16; **ordinary,** *per l'ordinario,* 12.49;
ordinarily, *per ordinario,* 19.73

outside, *externo,* 26.105; **outsider,** *esterno,* 3.10. *See also* external;
foreign

overcome, *superare,* 6.24 (2×), 7.29, 8.35, 10.44, 12.50, 18.69, 20.85
(2×), 26.104; **overcome,** *vincere,* 4.18. For *vincere, see also* conquer; win

parricide, *parricida,* 8.37. *Cf.* father; patrimony

parsimony, *parsimonia* (L), 16.62 (T); **parsimony,** *parsimonia,* 16.63,
16.64

partisan, *partigiano,* 7.29, 20.83, 20.84; **partisan,** *del parte,* 7.28; **with partisan zeal,** *partigianamente,* 6.24

party, *parte,** 7.28, 7.31, 11.47 (3×), 13.55, 20.84 (3×)

past (n.), *adrieto,* 12.50, 14.60; **preceding** (n.), *adrieto,* 25.99; **above,** *della passata,* 11.46; **past ones,** *le passate,* 24.96; **past** (adj.), *passato,* 7.30; **last,** *passato,* 26.104; **pass,** *passare,* 8.36; **come,** *passare,* 21.89

path, *via,* 5.21, 6.22(3×), 6.23, 6.24, 7.25, 7.27, 8.34, 11.47, 16.64, 25.100. *Cf.* way

patrimony, *patrimonio,* 8.36, 17.67. *Cf.* father; parricide

patron, *patrone,* 5.20, 12.49, 12.50

peace, *pace,* 6.23, 12.48, 14.59 (2×), 17.65, 18.71, 20.85; **to peace,** *pacifica,* 7.29 (2×); **peace treaty,** *pace,* 18.69; **bring to peace,** *pacare,* 19.79; **peaceful,** *pacifico,* 8.37, 14.60

people, *populo, passim;* **people,** *universale,* 9.41, 19.73, 19.75, 19.76

perform, *operare,* 12.51

philosopher, *filosofo,* 19.75

physician, *fisico,* 3.12

piety, *pietà,* 26.105; **pious,** *pietoso,* 21.88; **pious,** *pia* (L), 26.103. *See also* mercy

plan (v.), *disegnare,* 6.22, 7.31, 20.86, 23.95; **sketch,** *disegnare,* ED.4; **plan** (n.), *disegno,* 6.22, 7.32, 8.34, 23.94, 25.99; **according to plan,** *a proposito,* 20.84; **purpose,** *proposito,* 13.55; **regard,** *proposito,* 23.94

pleasure* (n.), *piacere,* 21.89

plebs, *plebe,* 10.43 (2×), 12.51

pledge (v.), *obligare,* 3.15. *See also* oblige

poison (n.), *veleno,* 13.57

policy, *partito,* 8.35, 19.80; **policy,** *parte,** 3.11, 3.12, 9.38; **policy,** *termine,** 23.94

pontiff, *pontefice,* 7.33, 11.46 (2×), 25.100, 25.101; **pontificate,** *pontificato,* 11.46, 11.47, 19.82. *Cf.* pope

poor, *povero,* 3.10 (2×), 16.63, 16.64, 16.65; **poverty,** *povertà,* 16.65

pope, *papa,* 2.7, 3.14, 3.15, 3.16, 7.27, 7.28, 7.31 (3×), 7.32, 7.33 (4×), 8.37, 11.45, 11.46 (7×), 11.47, 12.52, 13.54 (2×), 16.63, 21.91, 25.100; **papacy,** *papato,* 7.33, 16.63. *Cf.* pontiff

power, *potenzia,* 3.12 (2×), 3.15, 3.16, 4.19, 5.20, 7.27, 7.29, 7.31, 7.33, 25.98; **power,** *potestà,* 7.29; **power,** *potente,* 3.11 (4×), 3.12 (2×), 3.15 (2×), 10.43, 11.46, 13.54, 21.8; **power,** *po-*

tentato, 11.45 (3×), 19.72; **power,** *potentiae* (L), 13.57; **power,**
imperio, 11.45, 19.79, 21.88; **powerful,** *potente,* 3.11 (5×), 3.12,
3.15 (2×), 3.16 (2×), 6.25, 7.30, 7.31, 10.44, 11.45, 11.47,
19.73, 19.75, 19.76, 20.84, 21.90 (2×); **impotent,** *impotente,*
7.29. For *imperio, see also* empire

praetor, *pretore,* 8.34; **praetorian,** *pretoriani,* 19.78

praise (v.), *laudare,* 3.14, 14.60, 18.71, 20.86, 20.87; **praise** (v.), *lau-*
dantur (L), 15.61 (T); **praise** (n.), *laude,* 11.47, 14.59, 15.61,
19.77; **praiseworthy,** *laudabile,* 15.62, 18.68

pray, *pregare,* 26.102. *See also* beg

preach, *predicare,* 18.71

prelate, *prelato,* 11.47

prepare, *preparare,* 7.26, 21.91, 26.104; **preparation,** *preparazione,*
9.41, 17.66

pretext, *colore,* 19.78. *See also* color

priest, *prete,* 12.52

prince,★ *principe,* ED.3, ED.4 (3×), 1.5 (2×), 1.6, 2.6 (2×), 2.7, 3.8
(2×), 3.9 (2×), 3.10, 3.12, 3.16, 4.17 (4×), 4.18 (3×), 5.20, 5.21
(3×), 6.21, 6.22 (4×), 6.23, 6.25 (2×), 7.25, 7.26 (4×), 7.27,
7.32, 8.34 (3×), 8.37, 8.38, 9.38, 9.39 (5×), 9.40 (5×), 9.41
(3×), 9.42 (4×), 10.42, 10.43, 10.44 (6×), 11.45, 12.48 (2×),
12.49 (3×), 12.50 (2×), 12.52, 13.55, 13.57, 14.58 (5×), 14.59
(2×), 14.60 (2×), 15.61 (4×), 15.62, 16.63 (2×), 16.64 (5×),
16.65, 17.65 (2×), 17.66 (4×), 17.67 (3×), 17.68 (2×), 18.68,
18.69 (7×), 18.70 (5×), 18.71 (3×), 19.71, 19.72 (3×), 19.73
(5×), 19.74 (4×), 19.75 (2×), 19.76 (4×), 19.77, 19.78 (2×),
19.79 (2×), 19.81 (3×), 19.82 (4×), 20.83 (2×), 20.84 (2×),
20.85 (8×), 20.86 (3×), 20.87, 21.87, 21.88 (2×), 21.89 (2×),
21.90 (4×), 21.91 (2×), 22.92 (3×), 22.93 (3×), 23.93, 23.94,
23.95 (6×), 24.96 (3×), 24.97, 25.99 (2×), 26.101, 26.102 (2×),
26.104, 26.105; **prince,** *principem* (L), 14.58 (T), 21.87 (T);
princes, *principes* (L), 15.61 (T), 22.92 (T), 24.96 (T); **princes,**
principibus (L), 18.68 (T), 20.83 (T)

principality,★ *principato,* 1.5 (2×), 2.6 (2×), 3.7, 3.8 (2×), 3.9,
4.17, 4.19, 6.21, 6.22, 6.23 (2×), 7.32, 8.34, 8.35 (2×), 8.37,
9.39 (6×), 9.40, 9.41, 10.42, 11.45 (2×), 12.48, 13.57 (2×),
15.61, 16.64, 19.73, 19.76, 19.80 (2×), 19.82 (5×), 20.84, 20.85
(2×), 24.96, 24.97; **principality,** *principatus* (L), 1.5 (T), 2.6 (T),
3.7 (T), 5.20 (T), 6.21 (T), 7.25 (T), 8.34 (T), 9.38 (T), 10.42 (T),

11.45 (T); **principal,** *principale,* 11.46, 12.48, 17.67; **principate,** *principato,* 19.76, 19.82

progress, *progresso,* 3.12, 12.49, 12.50, 12.51, 12.52. *See also* step

property,★ *roba,* 17.66, 17.67 (3×), 19.72 (2×). *Cf.* belongings

proportion, *proporzione,* 6.25, 14.58

protection, *difesa,* 19.73

proud, *superbo,* 15.62

proverb, *proverbio,* 9.41

province,★ *provincia,* 3.9 (2×), 3.10, 3.11 (4×), 3.12 (3×), 3.13 (2×), 3.14, 3.16, 4.17, 4.19, 5.20, 5.21, 7.29, 7.30, 11.45, 14.59 (2×), 19.81, 20.86, 26.105; **inhabitant of a province,** *provinciale,* 3.8, 3.11. For *provincia, see also* country

prudence, *prudenzia,* 3.13, 13.57, 17.66, 21.90, 21.91, 22.92, 23.95 (2×), 24.96, 25.98, 25.101; **prudent,** *prudente,* 3.12, 6.22 (2×), 7.27, 10.44, 15.62, 16.63, 18.69, 19.75, 23.94 (2×), 25.100, 26.102; **most prudent,** *prudentissimo,* 12.51; **very prudent,** *prudentissimo,* 23.93, 23.95; **prudently,** *prudentemente,* 24.96

public (adj.), *publico,* 10.43; **public** (n.), *pubblico,* 10.43

punish, *punire,* 3.9, 19.79, 21.89; **punishment,** *pena,* 12.49, 17.67, 19.73

purge, *purgare,* 7.30

pusillanimous, *pusillanimo,* 15.62, 19.72; **pusillanimity,** *pusillanimità,* 9.40. *Cf.* intent; magnanimous

quality, *qualità,* ED.4, 6.25, 7.28, 9.42, 10.42, 12.47, 15.61, 16.62, 17.65, 17.68, 18.70 (2×), 18.71, 19.71, 19.77, 19.80, 19.85, 20.84, 20.85, 21.88, 21.90, 21.91, 25.99 (3×)

quarrel, *scandolo,* 11.46

queen, *regina,* 12.50

question (v.), *dubitare,* 8.37. *See also* doubtful; fear; hesitate

rank, *grado,* 4.17, 7.26, 8.34 (3×), 8.35, 8.36, 9.40, 14.58, 16.64, 19.82, 22.92; not translated, 7.26. For *grado, see also* favor; grateful

ransom, *taglia,* 12.53, 16.64. *Cf.* taxes

rapacious, *rapace,* 19.72; **rapine,** *rapina,* 15.61, 17.67. *See also* robbery

read, *leggere,* ED.4, 14.60 (2×), 19.75; **reading,** *lezione,* ED.3. *Cf.* write

reason★ (n.), *ragione,* 4.18 (3×), 4.19, 14.60, 20.84, 21.89, 21.91; **reason** (v.), *ragionare,* 2.6, 6.22, 8.34, 11.45, 12.48, 14.59, 19.81; **reasonable,** *ragionevole,* 2.7, 3.15, 3.16, 4.17, 7.26, 14.58; **reasonably,** *ragionevolmente,* 10.44; **reasoning,** *ragionare,* 2.6, 12.48. For *ragione, see also* kind; *cf.* discussion

rebel (v.), *rebellare,* 3.8, 4.17, 17.68, 19.81; **rebel** (v.), *defecit* (L), 4.16 (T); **rebellion,** *rebellione,* 3.8, 4.18, 4.19, 5.21, 7.28

regard,* *respetto,* 7.31. *See also* caution; concern; respect

reign (v.), *regnare,* 8.35; **reign** (n.), *regno,* 21.88. *See also* rule; *cf.* command; empire; emperor; imperial; king

religion, *religione,* 8.35, 11.45, 18.70 (2✕), 21.88; **religious,** *religioso,* 15.62, 18.70. *Cf.* sect

remedy (n.), *remedio,* 3.9, 3.10 (3✕), 3.12, 7.31, 7.32, 8.38, 9.41, 10.44, 12.51, 14.60, 19.73, 24.97, 25.98, 26.105; **remedy** (v.), *rimediare,* 3.10, 3.12 (2✕)

renew, *rinnovare,* 8.38. *Cf.* innovate

republic,* *republica,* 1.5, 2.6, 5.21, 8.34 (2✕), 12.49 (2✕), 12.50 (2✕), 12.52, 13.57, 15.61

reputation,* **repute,** *reputazione,* 3.12, 3.13, 3.14, 7.28, 7.29 (2✕), 7.31, 9.39 (2✕), 9.40, 10.44, 12.51 (2✕), 12.52 (3✕), 12.53 (3✕), 13.55, 13.56, 16.64, 18.71, 19.76, 19.79, 20.85, 21.88, 26.105; **reputed,** *reputarsi,* 22.92; **reputed,** *reputato,* 19.72 (2✕), 19.76. *Cf.* believe; fame; opinion

respect, *rispetto,* 4.17; **respect,** *respetto,* 3.11, 19.82, 21.90, 24.97. *See also* concern; hesitate; regard

revenge, *vendetta,* 3.11, 5.21, 26.105. *Cf.* avenge

revere, *reverire,* 7.32, 19.72, 19.79, 26.104; **reverence,** *riverenzia,* 23.94; **reverent,** *reverente,* 19.78

review (v.), *discorrere,* 8.38, 13.57, 19.77, 20.86. *See also* discourse; discuss

reward (n.), *premio,* 21.91; **reward** (v.), *premiare,* 16.63, 21.89

rich, *ricco,* 8.34, 22.93; **riches,** *ricchezze,* 25.99. *See also* wealth

right, hereditary, *iure hereditario,* 19.77, 19.80, 19.82. For *hereditario, see also* hereditary; for *iure, cf.* just

robbery, *rapina,* 17.66, 19.79; **robbery,** *latrocinio,* 7.29. For *rapina, see also* rapine; violence

rule (v.), *reggere,* 10.42, 10.43, 19.74, 20.84, 20.85; **rule** (v.), *regnare,* 16.64, 19.78; **rule** (n.), *regola,* 3.14, 3.16, 9.40, 23.95; **give rules,** *regolare,* ED.4. For *regnare, see also* reign; *cf.* command; emperor; empire; imperial; king

sad, *tristo,* 13.54

safe, *securo, sicuro,* 13.55, 17.66, 21.91, 26.105. *See also* secure

satisfy, *satisfare,* 3.8, 3.10, 7.30, 9.39, 19.73 (2✕), 19.74, 19.76 (2✕), 19.77, 19.78 (2✕), 19.80, 19.81 (3✕); **satisfaction,** *satisfazione,* 21.89

scorn (n.), *sdegno,* 14.58. *See also* indignation; *cf.* dignity; disdain

secret, *secreto,* 8.37 (2×); **secretive,** *secreto,* 23.94; **secretly,** *secretamente,* 8.36, 19.73; **secretary,** *secretis* (L), 22.92 (T)

secure, *securo, sicuro,* 3.10, 3.14, 4.19 (2×), 5.20, 5.21, 6.25, 7.32, 8.37 (2×), 11.45, 12.48, 13.57, 14.58, 20.86, 20.87, 24.96; **secure,** *assicurato,* 7.30; **securely,** *securamente, sicuramente,* 3.9, 7.27, 12.51, 20.83, 20.86; **security,** *securtà, sicurtà,* 6.23, 7.26, 15.62, 19.74, 19.75, 19.81, 20.83, 20.85, 24.97; **secure** (v.), *assicurare,* 3.8, 3.14, 5.21, 7.29, 7.30, 7.31, 7.32, 8.38 (3×), 9.39 (2×), 9.41, 10.44, 12.52, 19.73, 19.75, 24.96, 24.97; **secure** (v.), *prendere,* 12.51. *See also* safe

Senate, *Senato,* 8.34, 17.68 (3×), 19.78 (3×), 19.79, 19.81; **senator,** *senatore,* 8.34. *Cf.* father

servant, *servo,* 4.17 (3×); **servant,** *servidore,* 8.36; **servant,** *servitore,* 14.58; **service,** *servizio,* 19.80; **servile,** *servo,* 26.102; **servile,** *servile,* 8.36; **servitude,** *servitù,* 5.21, 6.23, 8.36, 13.55. *Cf.* enslaved, homage

shadow, *ombra,* 9.39

shame, *vergogna,* 10.44, 24.96

Signor,* *signor,* 7.29. *See also* lord; *cf.* master

sin* (n.), *peccato,* 12.49 (2×)

site, *sito,* 14.59 (4×)

slow, *grave,* 17.66. *See also* grave

soldier (v.), *militare,* 8.36. *See also* fight

son, *figliuolo,* 3.16, 7.27, 8.37, 13.56, 14.58, 19.74, 19.75 (2×), 19.79, 19.80, 19.82. For *figliuolo, see also* child

sort, *sorte,* 26.102. *See also* chance

spare, *perdonare,* 19.78

spirit, *animo,* ED.4, 3.15, 6.23, 7.30, 7.32, 8.34, 8.35, 8.36, 9.40, 9.41, 10.44 (3×), 13.56, 17.66, 18.70 (2×), 19.73, 19.75, 19.76, 19.79, 19.80, 26.102, 26.105; **spirit,** *spirito,* 26.102; **spirited,** *animoso,* 8.35, 10.44, 11.46, 15.62; **spiritedness,** *animosità,* 19.72. For *animo, see also* intent; mind; *cf.* magnanimous; pusillanimous; for *animare, see also* inspire

spiritual, *spirituale,* 3.14. *Cf.* spirit

spokesmen, *oratori,* 21.89

state,* *stato,* ED.4, 1.5 (2×), 2.6, 2.7, 3.9 (3×), 3.10 (4×), 3.11 (3×), 3.12 (3×), 3.13 (2×), 3.15, 3.16, 4.16, 4.17 (6×), 4.18 (3×), 4.19 (4×), 5.20 (4×), 6.21, 6.22, 6.23, 7.26 (2×), 7.27 (5×),

7.31, 8.37, 8.38 (2×), 9.41, 9.42 (4×), 10.42, 11.45 (3×), 11.46, 12.48 (3×), 12.51, 12.52, 12.53, 14.58, 15.62 (2×), 17.66, 18.70, 18.71 (3×), 19.73, 19.74 (2×), 19.77, 19.78, 19.79, 19.82 (4×), 20.83 (3×), 20.84 (5×), 20.85 (2×), 20.86 (6×), 20.87 (2×), 21.88, 21.91 (2×), 22.93, 23.94, 23.95, 24.96 (3×), 24.97; **new states,** *nuovi,** 2.6; **state,** *regnum* (L), 24.96 (T)

step, *progresso,* 3.13, 7.27. *See also* progress

storm, *tempesta,* 24.97

strength, *fortezza,* 19.72, 19.81; **strength,** *virtù,* 6.22. For *fortezza, see also* fortress; for *virtù, see also* virtue

stroke, *tratto,* 8.37 (2×), 8.38, 12.50

stupified, *stupido,* 7.30, 19.78

successor, *successore,* 4.17, 4.19, 7.31; **successor,** *successoribus* (L), 4.16 (T)

suitable, *conveniente,* 10.43, 17.67, 19.74, 21.91, 25.99; **to suit himself,** *a suo modo,* 7.30, 7.33, 9.39. *See also* convenience; fitting

support (n.), *favore,* 3.8, 3.11, 8.34, 8.35, 8.36, 9.39 (2×), 9.40 (3×), 19.76, 20.86; **in support,** *in favore,* 21.89, 21.90; **support** (v.), *favorire,* 12.52 (2×), 20.86 (3×), 26.102. For *favore, favorire, see also* favor

suspect (adj.), *sospetto, suspetto,* 3.9, 3.16, 14.58, 20.83 (2×), 20.84, 20.85 (2×), 21.89. For *sospetto, see also* anticipation; fear

tax, *dazio,* 3.9, 16.63; **taxes,** *taglie,* 21.91, 26.102; **rigorous with taxes,** *fiscale,* 16.63. *Cf.* ransom

teach, *insegnare,* 14.59, 18.69; **teacher,** *precettore,* 6.23, 18.69; **teaching,** *precetto,* 7.27, 18.69, 20.84

tell,* *narrare,* 12.49, 19.80, 21.89

temporal, *temporale,* 3.14, 11.45 (2×), 11.46, 12.52 (2×); **temporize,** *temporeggiare,* 2.6

terrible, *terribile,* 17.67, 26.104; **terrifying,** *che lo sbigottisce,* 19.73

test, *esperienzia,* 9.42. *See also* experience; experiment

Testament, *Testamento,* 13.56. *Cf.* testimony

testimony, *testimone,* ED.3, 26.104. *Cf.* Testament

think, *pensare, passim;* **thought,** *pensiero,* 14.58, 14.59

thrust* (n.), *impeto,* 19.72. *See also* impetuosity

title, *titulo,* 19.78

town, *terra,* 10.43 (3×), 12.53 (2×), 14.59, 20.83, 20.84. *See also* land

troops, *genti, gente,* 12.50, 13.55, 25.100. *See also* man

trouble (v.),* *scandolo,* 3.12

trust (v.), *confidare*, 20.85, 22.93; **trust** (v.), *fidarsi*, 7.27, 7.29, 9.42, 12.49, 14.58, 20.87, 22.93; **distrust** (v.), *diffidenzia*, 20.83. For *confidare, see also* confidence; *cf.* faith; believe

true, truth, *vero*, *3.8, 9.41, 12.49, 15.61, 17.68, 21.89 (2×), 23.94 (2×), 23.95, 25.98, 26.104; **truth,** *verità,* *5.20, 15.61, 23.94

tumult, *tumulto*, 4.19, 7.28, 11.47 (2×)

uncle, *zio*, 8.35. *Cf.* nephew

undertaking, *impresa*, 8.37, 10.43, 26.103, 26.104. *See also* campaign; enterprise

union, *unione*, 7.29, 11.46; **disunion,** *disunione*, 7.29; **unity,** *unità*, 7.29

unite, *unire*, 10.44, 17.65, 20.84, 23.95; **united,** *unito*, 4.18, 13.55, 17.65, 17.67, 23.95; **united,** *uniti*, 4.19; **disunite,** *disunire*, 12.48

universal, *universale*, 3.9. *See also* community; general

unlike, formed unlike, *disforme*, 19.75, 19.82. *See also* disparate; *cf.* conform

uprising, *impeto*, 20.87. *See also* impetuousity

upset (v.), *turbassinarsi*, 7.27

use, *utile*, 4.18; **use,** *utilità*, 20.85; **useful,** *utile*, 3.11, 13.54, 13.56, 14.59, 15.61, 18.70, 19.76, 20.86, 21.89 (2×), 22.93; **useful,** *utilia* (L), 20.83 (T); **useless,** *inutile*, 3.11, 12.48, 13.54, 19.82, 22.92; **useless,** *inutilia* (L), 20.83 (T). *See also* utility

usurper, *usurpatore*, 19.72

utility, *utilità*, 8.38, 17.67, 20.85. *See also* use

variation, variability, *variazione*, 18.70, 25.98, 25.99 (2×), 25.100. *See also* change; instability

veneration, *venerazione*, 6.24; **venerable,** *venerando*, 11.47, 17.67, 19.77

vent, *sfogare*, 9.39, 19.76. *See also* satisfy

vice, *vizio*, 2.7, 15.62 (3×), 16.64

victor, *vincitore*, 4.18, 4.19, 13.54, 24.97; **victor,** *victor* (L), 21.90; **victory,** *vittoria*, 4.18 (2×), 4.19, 12.50, 13.55, 14.60, 21.90; **most victorious,** *vittoriosissimo*, 9.41. For *vincitore, see also* win; *cf.* conquer; overcome

violate, *sforzare*, 12.53

violence, *violenzia*, 8.34, 9.39, 25.99; **violent,** *rovinoso*, 25.98

virtue, *virtù*, 1.6, 3.13, 4.19, 6.22 (4×), 6.23 (4×), 6.24, 6.25, 7.26 (4×), 7.27, 7.31 (2×), 8.34 (2×), 8.35 (3×), 8.37, 9.39, 11.45, 11.47, 12.51, 12.53, 13.55, 13.56, 13.57 (2×), 14.58, 15.62, 16.63, 17.67 (2×), 17.68, 19.75, 19.77, 19.78 (2×), 19.82,

21.91, 24.97, 25.98, 25.99, 26.102 (3×), 26.103, 26.104 (3×), 26.105; **virtue,** *virtute* (L), 6.21(T); **virtuous,** *virtuoso,* 6.22, 7.27, 12.49, 12.51, 21.91, 24.96, 26.102; **of virtue,** *virtuoso,* 6.23; **most virtuous,** *virtuosissimo,* 12.51; **virtuously,** *virtuosamente,* 16.63; **most virtuously,** *virtuosissimamente,* 12.51. For *virtù, see also* strength

wanton, *licenzioso,* 25.98. *See also* license

war, *guerra,* 3.12 (2×), 3.13, 3.15 (2×), 3.16, 8.37, 12.48, 12.49 (2×), 12.50, 12.51 (2×), 12.52, 13.54, 13.56, 14.58, 14.59 (3×), 14.60, 16.63 (3×), 20.85, 20.87, 21.88 (2×), 21.89, 24.97, 26.103, 26.104; **war,** *bellum* (L), 26.103; **war,** *bello* (L), 21.90; **very warlike,** *bellicosissimo,* 19.80

way,* *via,** 4.18, 21.90. *Cf.* path

weak, *debole,* 3.9, 3.14, 9.42, 11.46, 12.52, 20.84, 21.88; **weaken,** *indebolire,* 3.11, 7.28; **weaken,** *fare debole,* 3.14; **weaken,** *enervare,* 13.57; **weakness,** *debolezza,* 20.85, 26.104

wealth, *ricchezza,* 22.93 (2×). *See also* rich

well-being, *bene essere,* 7.29, 12.48, 15.62

wicked, *tristo,* 17.67, 18.69. *See also* bad

will, *arbitrio,* 25.98, 26.103; **will,** *voglia,* 19.77; **will,** *volontà,* 7.26, 7.28, 9.42; **good will,** *benevoluto,* 2.7; **good will,** *benivolenzia,* 19.73, 19.74; **show good will,** *essere benivolo,* 19.74; **willingly,** *volentieri,* 3.8, 3.11, 14.58; **willing,** *volonteroso,* 10.44; **at his will,** *ad votum* (L), 18.70

win, *vincere,* 9.40, 12.51 (4×), 12.52, 13.54 (2×), 13.55 (3×), 13.56, 16.64, 18.71, 21.89 (3×), 21.90 (5×), 25.101; **win over,** *guadagnarsi,* 4.18, 7.31 (3×), 20.85; **winner,** *vincitore,* 21.89, 21.90. For *vincere, vincitore, see also* conquer; defeat; victory; for *guadagnarsi, see also* gain

wise, *savio,* 3.12, 3.13, 9.42, 13.55, 13.57 (2×), 14.60, 17.68, 19.74, 20.84, 20.85, 21.90, 22.92, 23.94, 23.95 (2×); **wisdom,** *sapere,* 11.46; **wisdom,** *sapienza,* 16.65

woman, *donna,* 17.66, 19.72, 25.101 (2×). *Cf.* effeminate; Madonna

word, *parola,* ED.4, 17.66

work (n.), *opera,* ED.3, ED.4; **work** (v.), *operare,* 14.58, 21.88, 25.99 (2×); **act,*** *operare,* 12.51, 18.70. For *opera, see also* deed; for *operare, see also* employ

world, *mondo,* 3.9, 18.70, 18.71, 19.79, 19.81; **worldly things,** *cose del mondo,* 10.44, 25.98

worthy, *degno,* ED.3; **most worthy,** *valentissimo,* 22.92; **prove wor-**

thy, *meritare*, 6.25; **be worthy,** *riuscire valente*, 12.50; **be worthy,** *valsere*, 20.87. For *degno, meritare, see also* bought; deserve; merit; *cf.* dignity; disdain; indignation

write, *scrivere*, 6.25, 8.36, 14.60 (2×), 15.61 (3×), 18.69, 19.78; **written above,** *soprascritto*, 19.82, 20.84, 24.96; **mentioned above,** *soprascritto*, 2.6, 15.62, 16.62, 18.70 (2×), 19.71; **given above,** *soprascritto*, 3.14; **writer,** *scrittore*, 14.59, 17.67, 18.69

young, *giovane*, 25.101; **young,** *gioventù*, 8.36

Bibliography

Baron, Hans. "Machiavelli: The Republican Citizen and the Author of *The Prince.*" English Historical Review 76 (1961): 217–53.

Berlin, Isaiah. "The Originality of Machiavelli." In Isaiah Berlin, *Against the Current.* New York: Viking Press, 1980, pp. 25–79.

Burckhardt, Jacob. *The Civilization of the Renaissance in Italy.* New York: Penguin Books, 1990.

Chabod, Federico. *Machiavelli and the Renaissance.* London: Bowes and Bowes, 1958.

DeGrazia, Sebastian. *Machiavelli in Hell.* Princeton: Princeton University Press, 1989.

Donaldson, Peter S. *Machiavelli and Mystery of State.* Cambridge: Cambridge University Press, 1988.

Fleisher, Martin, ed. *Machiavelli and the Nature of Political Thought.* New York: Atheneum, 1972.

Garver, Eugene. *Machiavelli and the History of Prudence.* Madison: University of Wisconsin Press, 1987.

Gilbert, Allan H. *Machiavelli's Prince and Its Forerunners: The Prince as a Typical Book de Regimine Principum.* Durham, N.C.: Duke University Press, 1938.

Gilbert, Felix. *History: Choice and Commitment.* Cambridge, Mass.: Harvard University Press, 1977.

Hale, J. R. *Machiavelli and Renaissance Italy.* New York: Collier Books, 1960.

Hulliung, Mark. *Citizen Machiavelli.* Princeton, N.J.: Princeton University Press, 1983.

Kahn, Victoria. *Machiavellian Rhetoric: From the Counter-Reformation to Milton.* Princeton: Princeton University Press, 1994.

Lefort, Claude. *Le travail de l'oeuvre Machiavel.* Paris: Gallimard, 1972.

Machiavelli, Niccolò. *The Prince.* Translated by Leo Paul S. de Alvarez. Irving, Texas: University of Dallas Press, 1980.

———. *Il Principe.* Edited by L. Arthur Burd. Oxford: Clarendon Press, 1891.

———. *Il Principe.* Edited by Federico Chabod and Luigi Firpo, 5th ed. Turin: Einaudi, 1966.

———. *Il Principe.* Edited by G. Lisio. Florence: Sansoni, 1899.

———. *Il Principe.* Edited by Luigi Russo. Florence: Sansoni, 1931.

———. *Il Principe e altri scritti.* Edited by Gennaro Sasso. Florence: La Nuova Italia, 1963.

————. *Il Principe e Discorsi*. Edited by Sergio Bertelli. Milan: Feltrinelli, 1960.

————. *Tutte le opere*. Edited by M. Martelli. Florence: Sansoni, 1971.

————. *Tutte le opere storiche e letterrarie di Niccolò Machiavelli*. Edited by Guido Mazzoni and Mario Casella. Florence: Barbera, 1929.

Mansfield, Harvey C., Jr. *Machiavelli's New Modes and Orders: A Study of the Discourses on Livy*. Ithaca, N.Y.: Cornell University Press, 1979.

————. *Machiavelli's Virtue*. Chicago: University of Chicago Press, 1996.

O'Brien, Conor Cruise. "The Ferocious Wisdom of Machiavelli." In Conor Cruise O'Brien, *The Suspecting Glance,* London: Faber and Faber, 1972.

Orwin, Clifford. "Machiavelli's Unchristian Charity." *American Political Science Review* 72 (1978), pp. 1217–28.

Parel, Anthony. *The Machiavellian Cosmos*. New Haven: Yale University Press, 1992.

————, ed. *The Political Calculus: Essays on Machiavelli's Philosophy*. Toronto: University of Toronto Press, 1972.

Pitkin, Hanna. *Fortune Is a Woman: Gender and Politics in the Thought of Niccolò Machiavelli*. Berkeley, Calif.: University of California Press, 1984.

Pocock, J. G. A. *The Machiavellian Moment*. Princeton, N.J.: Princeton University Press, 1975.

Quaglio, A. E. "Per il testo 'De Principatibus' di Niccolò Machiavelli." *Lettere Italiane* 19 (1967): 141–86.

Ridolfi, Roberto. *The Life of Niccolò Machiavelli*. Translated by Cecil Grayson. Chicago, Ill.: University of Chicago Press, 1963.

Sasso, Gennaro. *Niccolò Machiavelli: Storia del suo pensiero politico*. Bologna: il Mulino, 1980.

Saxonhouse, Arlene. *Women in the History of Political Thought, Ancient Greece to Machiavelli*. New York: Praeger, 1985.

Skinner, Quentin. *The Foundations of Modern Political Thought*. 2 vols. Cambridge: Cambridge University Press, 1978.

————. *Machiavelli*. New York: Hill and Wang, 1981.

Strauss, Leo. *Thoughts on Machiavelli*. Glencoe, Ill.: The Free Press, 1958.

————. "Niccolò Machiavelli." In Leo Strauss and Joseph Cropsey, eds., *History of Political Philosophy*. Chicago: University of Chicago Press, 1972.

Sullivan, Vickie B. *Machiavelli's Three Romes: Religion, Human Liberty, and Politics Reformed*. De Kalb, Ill.: Northern Illinois University Press, 1996.

Tarcov, Nathan. "Quentin Skinner's Method and Machiavelli's *Prince*." *Ethics* 92 (1982): 692–709.

Whitfield, J. H. *Discourses on Machiavelli*. Cambridge: Heffer, 1969.

———. *Machiavelli*. Oxford: Blackwell, 1947.

Index of Proper Names

References are solely to the text of *The Prince*, by chapter and page in this edition.

Egypt, VI 23; XXVI 102
Epaminondas, the Theban (d.362
    B.C.), XII 50

Fabius Maximus (Quintus Fabius
    Maximus Cunctator) (d.203 B.C.),
    the "delayer" in his tactics against
    Hannibal, XVII 68
Faenza, lord of (Astorgio Manfredi)
    (1488–1502), defeated by Cesare
    Borgia and strangled in Rome in
    1502, III 13
Faenza, VII 27, 28
Ferdinand the Catholic (1452–1516),
    also Ferdinand II of Aragon and V
    of Castile, who unified the king-
    dom of Spain; married Isabella I of
    Castile; drove the Moors out of
    Spain in 1492 and the Marranos in
    1501–2; drove the French out of
    the kingdom of Naples in 1504;
    became king of Naples in 1505,
    XII 53; XIII 54; XXI 88
Fermo, VIII 36, 37
Ferrara, duke of, Ercole d'Este (1431–
    1505), followed by his son Alfonso
    d'Este (1476–1534), II 7; III 13
Ferrara, XI 46; XIII 54
Filippo, Duke (Filippo Maria Vis-
    conti) (1392–1447), duke of Milan
    1412–47, XII 50
Florence, IX 41; XIX 74
Florentines, III 13; V 21; VII 31; XI
    45–46; XII 50–51; XIII 54; XVII
    65; XXI 91
Fogliani, Giovanni, leading citizen of
    Fermo, killed in 1502, VIII 36–37
Forlì, Madonna of (Caterina Sforza)
    (1463–1509), countess of Forlì,
    natural daughter of Galeazzo
    Sforza; married Girolamo Riario,
    count of Forlì, and after her hus-
    band was assassinated in 1488 held

that state until it was taken by Ces-
    are Borgia in 1500, III 13; XX 87
Forlì, XIII 55
France, king of, III 9; IV 17; VII 30;
    XI 45; XVI 63; XXV 100, 101
France (king of), III 9, 13, 15, 16; IV
    18; VII 28, 29, 30, 31; XXI 90;
    XXV 100
France (as Gaul), IV 19
France, kingdom or country of, III 9;
    IV 18, 19; VII 33; XIII 56, 57; XIX
    74, 79; XXI 88; XXV 99
French, III 16; VII 27–28, 29, 30, 31;
    XI 46, 47; XIII 54, 55, 56; XXVI
    105

Gaeta, VII 30
Gascony, III 9
Genoa, III 13
Genoa, battle of (1507), XXVI 104
Germans, XXVI 105
Germany X 43; XXV 99
Ghibelline sect, partisans of the Holy
    Roman Emperor, XX 84
Giovanna II (1373–1435), queen of
    Naples 1414–35, XII 50
Girolamo, Count (Girolamo Riario)
    (d.1488), count of Forlì, husband
    of Caterina Sforza; murdered in
    1488, XX 87
Goliath, XIII 56
Goths, XIII 57
Gracchi, the (Tiberius and Gaius
    Sempronius), brothers, tribunes of
    the plebs, lost their lives to their
    enemies in the Senate, Tiberius in
    133 and Gaius in 121 B.C., IX 41
Granada, XXI 88
Greece, III 10, 11, 12, 13; IV 19; V 20;
    VII 26; IX 41; XIII 54–55; XXI
    89; XXIV 97
Guelf sect, partisans of the pope, XX
    84

148